Violent No More

Domestic abuse by men has reached catastrophic proportions in this country. It refers not only to the use of physical violence in intimate relationships, but also emotional, psychological, or sexual abuse that is used to establish power and control over women in relationships.

Violent No More outlines positive, straightforward steps that men can take to recognize and change their own abusive behavior. It tells how to:

- Reject sexist beliefs that women are less significant and the cultural conditioning that condones violence

- Break through denial and take responsibility for violent behavior

- Find healthy ways of responding to conflict

- Monitor behavior to avoid reverting to old patterns once a new path has been started

---

"*Violent No More* is a wonderful book. In it is everything a batterer needs to know to change his abusive behavior. It also spells out for victims what they need to know about a batterer and his violent behavior. This book is hope for the hopeless—a real blueprint for living a non-violent life."
— **Diane Droz, ACSW, Family Advocacy Program Counselor**

"Men *can* stop their violence. Paymar's thoughtful, nuanced book shows how, step by step."
— **Allan Creighton, Co-founder of Oakland Men's Project and author of *Helping Teens Stop Violence***

VIOLENT
NO MORE

Helping Men End
Domestic Abuse

MICHAEL PAYMAR

Hunter
House

Hunter House Inc., Publishers
P.O. Box 2914
Alameda, CA 94501-0914

Library of Congress Cataloging-in-Publication Data
Paymar, Michael.
Violent No More : helping men end domestic abuse / Michael Paymar.
p. cm.
ISBN 0-89793-139-4 : $19.95 — ISBN 0-89793-117-3 (pbk.) : $10.95
1. Abusive men—Rehabilitation. 2. Wife abuse—Prevention. I. Title.
RC569.5.F3P38 1993
616.85'822—dc20   93-18003

ORDERING: Trade bookstores and wholesalers in the U.S. and Canada, please contact:

Publishers Group West
4065 Hollis Street, Box 8843
Emeryville CA 94608   Phone: (800) 788-3123 Fax: (510) 658-1834.

Special sales: Hunter House books are available at special discounts for sales
promotions, organizations, premiums, fundraising, and for educational use. For
details please contact:

Special Sales Department
Hunter House Inc., Publishers
P.O. Box 2914
Alameda, CA 94501-0914   Phone: (510) 865-5282 Fax: (510) 865-4295

Individuals: Hunter House books are available at most bookstores or can be
ordered directly from the publisher by calling toll-free: **1-800-266-5592**

Cover Design: Beth Hansen   Book design: *Qalagraphia*
Project Editor: Lisa E. Lee   Copyeditor: Rosemary Wallner
Production Manager: Paul J. Frindt
Marketing: Corrine M. Sahli   Promotion: Robin Donovan
Customer Service: Laura O'Brien
Publisher: Kiran S. Rana
Printed and bound by Publishers Press, Salt Lake City UT
Manufactured in the United States of America

9   8   7   6   5   4   3   First edition

Contents

Beyond Personal Change: Educating the
    Community
Staying on Course: Your Life-long Commitment
Conclusion

Preface

To the Men Courageous
Enough to Read This Book

I wrote *Violent No More: Helping Men End Domestic Abuse* for men who want to stop hurting the ones they love. It holds out a hand to men who have been and are violent in relationships with women, and helps them understand what is behind their violence, and how to change. It is a practical guide, based on years of working with men who have been violent, and written with the knowledge that most of these men were willing and ready to change—once they knew how.

Domestic abuse is defined as the use of physical violence in an intimate relationship. Domestic abuse includes emotional, psychological, and sexual abuse as well as any other behavior a person uses to control a partner. Thousands of women are killed and seriously injured by their partners every year. Violence in the home is lethal—and it is illegal. But even though society is finally saying that domestic abuse is unacceptable, it still occurs in about 25% of our homes.

This book is not only for men who have been violent in the past, but also for men who are concerned that their current behavior is hurting the ones they love. If you are violent, you know on some basic level your behavior is wrong. Fortunately, men who are violent can decide to change. If you are reaching out for help, that is the first step toward change. The next steps will not be easy, because ending violent and abusive behavior requires struggling with long-held beliefs and behaviors that will be difficult to give up.

Somehow and somewhere, men learn attitudes and behaviors that are destructive. The relationships of a man who abuses his partner are like a minefield: nobody knows when things might explode and all hell break loose. Living in this minefield causes terror and hurts the entire family. Inside, the man knows it does not have to be like this. All of us have the basic ability to experience fulfilling relationships that provide meaning and love in our lives.

In this book you will meet several men who have made major changes in their lives. You will read their stories and probably relate to some of them; others may shock you deeply. Yet most of these men did change, and they are living proof that men who have been violent in relationships *can* change.

You will also hear the stories of women who have been battered. Their experiences will help you understand the perspectives and feelings of women who have been beaten by their male partners. If you are not currently in a relationship, think about past relationships as you read these stories and apply what you learn to future relationships you may have.

In addition to reading this book, I encourage you to seek help from programs in your community that work to end domestic violence. You will need this support, because it is important to talk to people who have dealt with these issues firsthand. Overcoming violence and abuse in a relationship is hard work and it can be lonely and frustrating.

Much like the men you will meet in this book, you will go through certain stages in your journey back from violence, a process that may take weeks, months, or years. First, you will begin to understand the big picture: where did I learn this behavior? Second, you will apply the big picture to your own experiences. This stage may be difficult, because facing up to personal faults usually brings about resistance. Yet it is a necessary step. The third stage is more practical: you will put into practice what you have learned. Whether you are in a relationship or not, you will begin to see things differently as you apply some of the suggestions in this book to your life.

The book ends with a chapter on healing. If you agree with the direction this book takes you, I hope you will continue the process of change so your life becomes healthier and more fulfilling. Remember, change takes time, but it is your life and it is worth every little bit of effort that you make. I wish you luck and success in your journey.

Acknowledgments

I want to acknowledge and thank the women and men in my life who have helped shape my thinking about relationships, sexism, and men's violence. First, I owe an unpayable debt to battered women who have struggled to change our collective consciousness about the roots of violence against women. It is through their continuing struggle and commitment to ending violence that some day we may see a more egalitarian and peaceful world.

I also want to acknowledge my dedicated friends from the Duluth Domestic Abuse Intervention Project and the Women's Coalition in Duluth, Minnesota, who have made a difference by working to end violence in our community. Their courage and unceasing dedication have permanently improved the lives of many in that city. Their efforts have provided a guiding light to many communities around the world.

I owe a special debt of gratitude to the men and women who volunteered to share their life experiences for this book.

I want to acknowledge and thank my partner Susan Aske-lin. Susan edited the manuscript, gave me constant encouragement and, early in our relationship, challenged me to truly understand the impact of sexism on women.

My family, Mandy, Frieda, Jim, Leslie, Jason, and Nicole, have been especially supportive of this endeavor.

I want to thank my friend and colleague Ellen Pence for her review and critical feedback. I continue to marvel at her tireless work on behalf of battered women, and the incredible contribution she has made in this field.

Finally, I want to thank Mardi Steinau, Allan Creighton, Lisa Lee, and Kiran Rana for their thoughtful critiques of the many drafts of my manuscript.

Violent No More

An Important Note
to the Reader

The material in this book is intended to provide a guide for men dealing with the issues of domestic abuse. Every effort has been made to provide accurate and dependable information and the contents of this book have been compiled in consultation with other professionals. However, the reader should be aware that professionals in the field may have differing opinions, and legal policies may differ from state to state and are changing constantly. The publisher, author, and editors cannot be held responsible for any error, omission, professional disagreement, or outdated material.

The ideas, procedures, and suggestions contained in this book are designed to encourage men to work with their personal violence and abusive behavior, but are not intended to replace a professional program. If you have any questions or concerns about applying the information in this book, please consult a domestic abuse intervention program or a licensed therapist. The author and publisher assume no responsibility for any outcome of the use of these materials individually or in consultation with a professional or group.

This book is written in a style that addresses the violent behavior of men in relationships and marriages with women, since that is the main focus of the author's work. However, most of the ideas, techniques, and processes will also apply to other intimate and familial relationships.

The persons and events described in the interviews in this book are real, but their names have been changed to protect their privacy and their families. The persons and events described in the group sessions quoted in this book are often composites, based on real people and events, but their names have also been changed for protection.

The numbers in parentheses in the text refer to endnotes, found on page 189.

Introduction

- Every fifteen seconds a woman is beaten by her husband or boyfriend in the United States.

- Thirty percent of all female homicide victims are killed by a partner or former partner.

- One out of every four men will use violence against a partner at some time in their relationship.

- Children are present during 80% of the assaults against their mothers.

No community is immune to domestic violence. Emergency rooms sew up cuts, fix broken bones, and treat the bruises. Overcrowded shelters provide temporary safety and emotional support to victims. Offenders get arrested and protection orders are issued, but the courts are already overbusy and the jails overcrowded. And the violence continues.

When does it stop? How will it stop? And finally, whose responsibility is it to end this cycle of violence?

Laws alone will not end domestic abuse. Men must stop the excuses and end the silence. Ultimately, men must make personal decisions about how they want to conduct their lives. Men need to understand the origins of their violence against women and commit to ending it in their own lives.

Over the years, I have talked to hundreds of violent men. Most men who hit once usually hit again. Also, most men said that their abusive behavior escalated until they finally got arrested or decided to seek help.

Men who are violent or abusive often project an attitude of not needing or not wanting to change. Deep down, most of them know that something is not right. They start new relationships with high expectations only to see their abusive behavior tear the relationship apart. They medicate themselves with drugs, alcohol, and cynicism about life and relationships. Their friendships with other men are frequently superficial. They see their children acting out in inappropriate ways because of what is happening at home, and they don't know what to do. They see their partners, who once loved them, turn away in anger and in fear. All too often they end up alone, out of touch with their own feelings and cut off from the company and affection of others, pretty much trapped . . . .

If this description sounds familiar, I hope you will continue reading.

There is no single profile of a man who is violent. Abusers are rich, middle class, and poor, blue collar and white collar, old and young. Some grew up with violence in the home and others did not. Some have college degrees and others dropped out of school. Some batter when they are drunk and some when they are sober. They come from all races, religions, and cultures.

Men are not naturally violent, but they learn that violence is an appropriate male response to settling disagreements. Men also learn that violence can bring a feeling of power. However, men can reject the cultural conditioning that spawns this violence. They can reject sexist beliefs that women are less significant than men. We can teach our sons and daughters that men and women are equal, that relationships should be respectful, and that violence is not an acceptable way to resolve conflicts.

Why Write a Book for Men Who Batter?

A book like this can be a catalyst for personal change. By understanding how and why you got where you are, and by recognizing your own potential to change, you can begin a healthier life. Hurting others and yourself will lessen as you commit to this new beginning.

Back in the early 1970s I was very active in political and social causes. The women's movement was just beginning to blossom but, like many other men, at that time I failed to understand the rage and frustration women felt at men's attitudes and the institutional roadblocks women experienced in our society. My attitudes about women were not that different from the men I talked with in jail or in groups. Though I never battered, my sexism was real. I thought on some level that men were better or more competent than women. It was not until female friends confronted me that I began questioning my own beliefs and attitudes. At first, I became defensive. But then I decided to accept the confrontation not as criticism but as a challenge to look deeper. I eventually realized that my sexism was not only wrong but it also got in the way of friendships and my ability to be intimate in relationships with women.

At about this time in my life, I decided to get involved with a small group of men who were meeting to discuss issues related to sexism and violence against women. I had recently been elected to the Duluth City Council and chaired a public hearing on sexual violence. Many people testified, and many good ideas were presented. Still, I felt frustrated at our inability to do more about ending violence in our community.

At the same time, in 1980, several women in Duluth began organizing the Domestic Abuse Intervention Project. That year there was a particularly gruesome homicide. After years of being brutally beaten by her husband, a young woman shot her husband in the stomach with a shotgun. When the paramedics arrived the man was literally in two parts. This incident and a growing concern about domestic abuse prompted an otherwise resistant justice system to listen to the organizers.

The Project sought to change the way the criminal justice system (law enforcement officers) and human service providers (social workers) responded to domestic assault cases. Police began arresting offenders, rather than attempting mediation between the couple or simply separating people by asking one party to leave for the night—because too often the man came back and continued or escalated his violence. The courts got tougher, but they also offered offenders an opportunity to change their behavior by going to counseling or domestic abuse classes.

When the project began, ten men in Duluth were chosen to counsel men in jail after arrests had taken place. Because I had taken a public stance and expressed interest in putting my energies into confronting violence in the community, the organizers invited me and nine other men to a meeting. They asked us if we would be willing to meet with men who were arrested under the new arrest law in Duluth. I now felt I had an opportunity to really help. I went to the jail in the early morning, met with men, and listened to their stories. I tried to get them to see the impact their violence was having on their families and the destructiveness of it. I talked about our program and the help we offered.

Most of the men who were arrested were shocked to be in jail. For many, a secret was finally being exposed. Some were honest with me and said they wanted help. Of course, sitting in the Duluth jail, an unfriendly place resembling Alcatraz, may have influenced their responses. Yet I felt most of these men truly felt remorse.

Others were angry and defiant, blaming their partners or the police. They would deal with their problems themselves, they said. They made it clear that they did not want or need any help from me.

Each of these men had fallen in love with someone and made a commitment to some kind of relationship. So, what had happened? How did the loving, smiling couples I saw in the wedding pages of our local newspaper become the angry, hurt faces I was now seeing in the cells of the Duluth jail?

The time I spent talking with these men in jail affected me profoundly and I started asking questions. Were these men so terribly different from me? I reached back into my childhood and began remembering the messages I had received about men and women. "Men should be in charge." "Men settle disagreements in a *manly* way—through fighting." "A man is king in his home, his castle." Was there a connection between these childhood messages and the prevalence of domestic abuse in our society?

The relationship between men's violence and what society tells us is the right way to be "male" became much clearer when

I began conducting groups outside the jail for men who battered. In the beginning, the majority of men in our groups were there because they were ordered by the court to attend. I remember feeling nervous as I walked into my first group. Would the men be angry at me because the court had forced them to be there? Would they talk honestly about their abusive behavior? Would they want to change? Would they even listen to me?

My first group was held at an old community center in Duluth. At the start of the meeting, I asked the men to form a circle. They reluctantly carried or dragged their chairs to the middle of the room. Some looked angry, others bored—and we had not even begun. A few looked resigned to the situation and even seemed open to whatever was going to happen.

Most of the men were dressed casually, except for Don and Bradley who wore suits. Howard, 55, was the oldest man there. The rest were aged between 20 and 40. Some of the men had been in trouble with the law before, but for most this was a new and embarrassing experience. One man, Paul, had volunteered to attend. He said he did not want to be abusive anymore and felt he was losing his family.

I introduced myself and told the group I realized that many of them did not want to be there, but I hoped they would be open to what the program had to offer. I said that sometimes something bad or uncomfortable has to happen before we are ready to make changes in our lives. I said I wanted them to know that I believed each of them *could* change—if he wanted.

Then I asked each man to introduce himself and explain why he was there. At first they were quiet, but gradually they started to talk.

As I thought about it afterward, I saw that the men had talked about their violence and relationships with women in three ways:

One group had stated that men and women have separate and distinct roles and that the man should be the head of the household. Their justification for this was the belief that "someone has to be in charge." This led to the further belief that if their partners challenged their authority, then some form of abusive behavior could be seen as a justifiable response.

Another group stated that their problems with their partners were mutual and the violence was a result of conflict in the relationship. They admitted that the violence was wrong, but believed that their partners had pushed or provoked them.

A third group—a couple of men, including Paul who had volunteered for this program—said clearly that their behavior was wrong. These men seemed truly disturbed by their actions. They were seeing the effects of their violence on their partners, families, and themselves. They seemed to have hit bottom. Their moral compass was not only indicating that their behavior was wrong, but now was guiding their desire to change.

The initial meetings of the group were challenging because the men had such varied beliefs about their behavior, coupled with a high degree of discomfort about having to be there. By the eighth meeting, however, most of them were talking freely. There was much disagreement and debate. That night, I wrote the word "SEXISM" on the board and asked what it meant to them and whether it had anything to do with domestic abuse. The following discussion took place (In the dialogue "Michael" is the author).

> **Don:** Sexism is when men treat women as unequal. You know, if women are paid less for the same job than men, that's sexism.
>
> **Paul:** I thinks it's a belief that men are superior to women. Most boys get taught that at an early age. If we believe that men are superior, then women are obviously inferior in some ways.

I asked how sexism might contribute to hitting a partner.

> **Paul:** Well, for some men, they think of their wives as property and you can do what you want with your own property.
>
> **Michael:** It's interesting that you speak of wives as property. Until the end of the nineteenth century there were actually laws

on the books setting out reasons why a man could beat his wife to discipline her. In fact, the saying "rule of thumb" actually came from a law that said a man could beat his wife with a stick no wider than his thumb.

Howard: Yeah, but don't you think things are changing with all this women's lib stuff? My wife works and she's free to do what she wants.

Michael: You mention women's lib. Why do you think women have organized women's liberation movements?

Howard: I suppose they don't believe that they are equal to men and maybe they're not in all respects. But I think some of this has gone too far.

Needless to say, we had a lively discussion that night. At the next session, several men told me that they had not really thought about the connections between men's violence to women and sexism.

In later groups we talked about domination, and why a woman would resist an unequal relationship with a man. Gradually, some men in the group began to recognize that they resorted to abuse and violence when their partners resisted being controlled. This was an important insight. Other men struggled with the ideas being discussed, while some of the men participated but remained quite unconvinced.

After six months, the first group of men had completed the program. Each said he had learned something from it, and all of them vowed they would not be violent again. Paul talked about how much his relationship with his partner had improved. I told him that I thought he had worked hard and that I appreciated his honesty. Bradley and his partner had split up, but he was sure that in his next relationship he would not make the same mistakes. We all said our good-byes, and I felt good about the experience.

Three months later I got a call from a local women's shelter telling me that two men had been arrested for assault the night

before. I got to the jail at 7 A.M. and was led down a line of cells
to the meeting room. The first man brought in for me to talk to
was Paul. He had smashed the headlights of his wife's car with
a baseball bat and threatened to kill her.

I was stunned and disappointed. I was so convinced that
Paul had turned the corner. Of all the men in my first group,
Paul seemed to have truly grasped the issues. He had talked
eloquently about men and women needing to respect each other,
that violence in a relationship was wrong. He had made a
commitment to handle conflicts with his partner differently
... and now here he was, in jail. I asked him to explain what
happened.

Paul said that he had not wanted to go to a party the night
before and that he had not wanted his partner, Robin, to go
either.

"I told Robin that I was too tired to go and that it would
be real nice if we both just stayed home together," he explained.
"She said that she had been counting on going for several weeks
and wanted to go. So I said go ahead, even though I didn't want
her to go. I was stewing all night long thinking that if she really
loved me she wouldn't have gone. And then I started wondering
why she wanted to go to the party so badly. It was two in the
morning before I heard the car drive up. I was so mad. I went
outside with a baseball bat and she ran back into the car. I
started screaming for her to get out, and when she didn't I
started smashing the car with the bat and threatened to kill her.
The neighbor called the police."

This early experience with Paul taught me that understanding the problem of violent and abusive behavior intellectually does not necessarily translate into changed behavior. There
is a saying frequently used in chemical dependency treatment:
"You've got to walk the walk, not just talk the talk." It means
that knowing what you need to change and saying that you
ought to change is not enough, you have to put the new behaviors or attitudes into practice as well. I had to keep remind-
ing myself that many of the men in our groups would return to
old, familiar territory and, unfortunately, would batter again.

In 1992, Melanie Shepard, a researcher at the University of
Minnesota, Duluth, examined the cases of 100 men who had
completed the counseling/education program at the Domestic
Abuse Prevention Project in 1985. She found that after a five
year period 40% of these men had either been arrested or had a
civil Order For Protection taken out against them for being
abusive. They had either abused the same woman they had
initially battered, or assaulted new partners.(1)

If 40% of the men completing our program were *reported* to
law enforcement or the courts, then it would be safe to assume
that at least half of the men arrested for domestic assault had
reverted to using abusive behavior despite counseling or the
threat of jail. However, the more groups I did, the more sure I
became that some of the men were making real and significant
changes. Sometimes the partners of these men reported marked
improvements in their behavior and attitude. And so I continued to believe in the work we were doing, and to have hope.

I chose to put my energies into this work because I think
we as men have a responsibility to end our violence. I believe
that it is simply inexcusable and a disgrace that women today
can still not feel safe among their friends, partners, colleagues
and lovers. Male violence has been our historical legacy. Our
prisons, battlefields, streets and homes have been marked by
our violence. And it needs to stop. I believe, to put it a little
simplistically, that it is much more "manly" to deal with our
own violence: to accept the challenge of struggling with it
without violating ourselves or others, and of releasing it so that
we are, truly, violent no more.

The First Step: Owning the Problem

Something motivated you to read this book. Perhaps a counselor, minister, rabbi, friend, or family member suggested it.
Maybe you are recognizing the pain you are causing your
family. Or perhaps you are concerned about behavior that is
scaring those around you—and yourself. What you read in the

chapters ahead may be hard to accept and it may cause you to become defensive. That is because taking the first step is never easy. The first step is owning the problem: acknowledging that it exists and taking responsibility for doing something about it.

Later in this book you will meet Andy, one of the first men to participate in the Domestic Abuse Intervention Project. He made significant changes in his life and is now working for our program. When I asked him what motivated him to change, he responded: "It was a combination of things—getting arrested, spending a night in jail, going to court, having my name in the paper, and being forced into groups. Even more, it was the fact that the secret was over. The lies about the black eyes, the cover-up on both our parts was over. Everyone knew—now the secret was exposed."

If there is hidden violence in your relationship, the first step toward change is deciding to end the secrecy. In fact, it is more than likely that people already know about your violence and abuse. It is difficult to keep that kind of secret from children, friends, family members, and neighbors, whether they acknowledge it or not.

Not too long ago, people who had alcohol or drug problems were regarded by many in society as failures. Today, celebrities and sports stars come forward, admit their problems, and publicly go into treatment centers. Much of the time society applauds rather than condemns. While I do not necessarily recommend getting up on a soap box on Main Street and declaring, "I batter my wife and I'm seeking help!" try to realize that society is much more accepting of people who acknowledge their mistakes honestly and look for solutions to their problems.

The Next Step: Getting Help

I advocate seeking help. I encourage men who abuse their partners to talk to other men, friends, family, clergy, and professionals about what has been happening in their lives. While some people will defend or support your abusive actions because they think that is what you want to hear, true friends, caring family members, and professionals will help you find ways to change and will support your efforts.

Many communities have domestic violence programs. If you have battered or are abusive, you may feel reluctant to go to such a program. You may be embarrassed or uncomfortable talking about such personal issues in a group setting. I urge you to take the risk and join. The other men in the group will have similar experiences and you will feel less alone.

Men and women should know that there usually are services available in their community. If you are a person of color there may be culturally sensitive programs that you would feel more comfortable attending. In Duluth, for example, the Native American community has designed specific groups for Native American men and women. If you are gay, there are specific organizations and resources available for you, too. (See Resources at the end of this book.) In different cities across the country groups have sprung up which provide culturally specific assistance and counseling on domestic abuse issues. If you have trouble locating these services, call a mental health agency, community center, or an information and referral number for help. Don't wait. Do it now.

The Domestic Abuse Intervention Project challenges beliefs and attitudes men have about women and teaches skills so men can remain nonviolent and noncontrolling in their relationships. The program takes the position that battering is intentional behavior. Its purpose is to control another person. The groups focus not only on ending violence, but also other abusive behavior.

For each group session, some men are court ordered to attend and others volunteer. I am always saddened by the many men who volunteer but then drop out after a short time. Many volunteer because their partner has told them to get help or get out. However, when things get a little better they quit, thinking that they have a handle on their problems. But there is no quick fix. When a man drops out of counseling after a few sessions he probably hasn't learned what he needs to learn to change his behavior. Frequently, the relationship worsens and his partner leaves. This can reinforce a sense of failure. Moreover, men who don't get help for themselves often repeat abusive behavior in new relationships.

Some counseling agencies agree to see men who batter on an individual basis. While this may be helpful, I am a strong advocate of the group process. The group provides an opportunity for men to learn from each other. In Minnesota, many counselors refuse to see men who have battered until after they have been through a group program.

Many men say they would prefer to go to couple or marriage counseling. They insist that the relationship cannot change unless both people get help. Unfortunately, some professionals in the mental health community support this assessment and provide marriage counseling. But, unless the violence has stopped and your partner feels safe with you, marriage counseling is inappropriate. Your partner will most likely be reluctant to discuss her true feelings in your presence because she is still afraid of you.

I asked Cassie, one of the women I interviewed for this book, about marriage counseling (her story appears in Chapter 2).

"We went to marriage counseling and it was a terrible experience," Cassie said. "The counselor said that I needed to be more accepting of him. I was angry because he was drinking a lot. The counselor said that on his days off, if he wanted to drink a case of beer in his own house that I should accept that.

"I was reluctant to bring up the violence and abuse, because I wasn't sure how my partner would react. That was the part of our problem that he didn't want known. The one time that I did mention the abuse it was basically discounted. When that happened, he felt totally validated. The counselor even said that I needed to be more sexually receptive to him and not be so critical of his faults."

The idea of marriage counseling is to sort through problems in the relationship. The goal is to heal and problem-solve. However, if a woman cannot talk freely in marriage counseling, how can the sessions be successful? Many practitioners believe that they have sufficient skills to ensure that violence will not occur after counseling. That position is not only naive but dangerous to battered women. I believe it is unethical and dangerous for mental health professionals to offer marriage counseling to couples where domestic violence has occurred unless the following has been done:

1. The man has successfully completed a domestic violence program.

2. The violence, threats, intimidation, and psychological abuse have ceased.

3. The woman has had contact with a battered women's program and has developed a plan to get help if her partner becomes abusive.

4. The counselor discusses with her privately the risks associated with marriage counseling and the counselor feels relatively sure that abusive acts will not take place as the result of these sessions.

Most communities have shelters, safe homes, and advocacy programs for battered women. They provide temporary safe lodging and may assist a woman in obtaining a protection order from the court. These programs usually provide education and support groups. I strongly encourage women to participate. The groups are a way to help each woman understand what has been going on in the relationship, and to help her realize that she is not responsible for the violence. Then she can sort out her options.

Some men are threatened when their partners attend these sessions. They think that the groups are anti-male, or that group members plot with her to end the relationship. This is not true. The groups are *anti-violence*. Many battered women experience confusion, pain, fear, and rage. Other women who have had similar experiences give them support. Men should support this as a healing process, and not ask about what their partner or other group members said. Respect your partner's need to participate and heal.

How to Use This Book

In the following chapters you will hear other stories of men who volunteered or were ordered by the court to participate in our counseling programs. Today, all of them are living violence-free lives and, while they continue to struggle with issues, they are a testimony to the possibility of change. You will also read more excerpts from groups that I conducted, alone and with others. To protect the privacy of the men and women quoted here all the names in this book have been changed, but their stories may sound familiar to you.

You will read examples of things you can do, or do differently, to avoid situations where you might be abusive. There are also a number of helpful exercises throughout the book. I invite you to complete these exercises. You may be surprised at what you learn about yourself. Use them to analyze yourself, to explore where you have been, and to set goals for the future.

Women who have lived and are living with men who have been violent will also find this book helpful, and certain parts are addressed directly to them. Similarly, counselors who work with men who batter will find the book useful in their work, both in the techniques and processes it describes and as something to share with men they work with.

Finally, whether you are a man or a woman, you may disagree with points that I make. That's okay. This book will expose you to some new ideas. Your initial reaction might be to slam the cover shut because you dislike what you are reading. Or you might feel that what is being said doesn't apply to you. My analysis of the roots of men's violence may make you uncomfortable. *But* ... please give it a chance—read on. If you complete the book I am confident it will truly guide you toward ending domestic abuse in your life.

1

The Roots of Men's Violence Against Women

Andy's Story — The Superman Myth —
How Our Culture Encourages Violence —
The Struggle for Equality — What Men
Expect From Relationships

Andy's Story

Andy was born in Duluth, Minnesota. He, like some of the men in this book, grew up with domestic violence in his family. He was arrested in 1982 for domestic assault and was ordered to attend our program. Andy has struggled to understand the roots of his violence. He has been violence-free for over ten years and now works with men who, like himself, have been abusive to women.

> I remember coming home from school and my father had my mother by the hair. It was obvious that she had been crying because her mascara was smeared and her face was all puffy. He had a knife in his hand and he said to me, "Do you want me to kill this bitch? Because I will!" I was crying and begging him not to hurt her.
>
> He battered her frequently and I never saw her fight back. She was always trying to accommodate him. Sometimes her attempts to appease him would work and sometimes they would piss him off more.

My brothers and I frequently got into fights, and my dad thought that was perfectly normal. If we complained or came to him, he would say that we had to settle it like men.

I got a lot of my attitudes about girls and women from my father, but mostly I think that society provided very negative messages about families in general. For me to get beat by a girl in a sports event was the ultimate in humiliation, and my father always told me that you shouldn't hit girls, yet he beat my mother. He died when I was eleven.

I met Debra in 1980 and we started to live together. The worst violence I remember was when Debra said something about me at this party and I got embarrassed. When we got outside I grabbed her and threw her to the ground and started pounding her head on the sidewalk. She was screaming and there was terror in her eyes. My brother ran over and tried to get me off of her. He said, "Andy, you're going to kill her!" I'm not sure if I would have, but I stopped.

I thought that Debra provoked my abuse. She would call me names or criticize my parenting abilities or say something that she knew would piss me off, and I felt totally justified in letting her have it.

I usually blamed Debra for the violence. When she would come home late I felt justified in hitting her. On some level I knew it was wrong to hit her, but I believed she brought it on herself. I always thought that if she would just stop resisting me and do as I said, she wouldn't get hit.

After being violent, I would try to get her to see that what I did wasn't that bad. I'd say, "You don't have any marks on you," or, "Other men would have done worse." If I'd slapped her, I'd say later, "Well, I didn't use a closed fist."

One time we got into a fight in the bedroom and I pushed her and she fell over the nightstand by the bed. She ended up with a broken arm and had to have a cast. A couple of weeks later, we were over at our friends' house, sitting around the table, and they asked what had happened to Debra's arm. She made up some story about tripping and falling. I was real uncomfortable and I got angry at her because I was embarrassed in front of our friends.

At the time, I never felt that Debra was afraid of me. If you had come into our house back then and asked me about her being afraid, I would have said, "Hell, no!" I mean, why would she sleep with me if she was afraid or why would she call me a fuckin' asshole if she was afraid? If she was afraid of me why would she say, "You're a sissy, go lay down by your fuckin' bowl by the dog. What are you going to do, hit a woman again?"

Debra was also violent with me. She was tough, and at the time both of us were into the bar scene. Sometimes she would throw things at me, slap me, or try and kick me. Actually, I was glad when she did that, because then I would feel totally justified in beating her up. There were times that I would goad her by getting in her face, calling her particular names so she would strike first. When she did, it would give me the green light to knock the hell out of her. After all, she hit me first. I was never afraid of her. Sometimes I would laugh at her after she hit me.

I rarely apologized unless the violence was real bad. When I apologized there was still this hint that it was her fault. I expected her to forgive me and I would get really angry when she wouldn't. When she didn't accept my apology, I would say, "You fuckin' bitch—you started this stuff, and now look at you!"

I never thought she would leave me, but she did. The police came to our house three times but never arrested me. When they came, I would be real calm and wouldn't show them my anger, and Debra would be real agitated. I would tell the police that it was her fault and that she started the fight. They would go over to her and tell her not to provoke me.

Finally they did arrest me, because they had told me to leave the house after an incident and I had come back. I was charged with assault. I was really mad at the police, the justice system, and Debra. I felt no one was listening to my side of the story and everyone was blaming me when I thought Debra was just as much to blame. I threatened Debra that if she didn't get the charges dropped I would really hurt her. She went to the city attorney, but they wouldn't drop the charges.

I was ordered into the batterers' program and was really resistant at first. I didn't think I belonged there. I would say in group,

"What about *her* violence? What am I supposed to do when she slaps me?" The counselors would challenge me to look at my violence and not to focus on her. It finally started to sink in and I realized that Debra didn't have to change for me to change.

After four or five groups something happened for me. It was actually freeing to take responsibility for my own behavior, and challenging to examine my beliefs. I began to enjoy going to groups and talking about this stuff with other men. Even though I started making changes, that wasn't enough to save my relationship with Debra. I guess too much had happened between us—too much pain and too much of my violence—for us to heal as a couple.

I waited a long time before I decided to get involved in a new relationship. I wanted to be sure that I had worked through my issues around wanting to control women. I also wanted to be absolutely sure that I would be nonviolent in any future relationship.

I told Beth, my current partner, about my past. It was a risk, but I felt she should know that I had battered Debra. I think it's important to be honest and accountable. Today, I'm constantly challenging my beliefs about men and women. In my current relationship I try to be aware of my body language, because I'm a big guy and I have a loud voice. I need to be careful about how I respond to my partner when I'm angry. I'll always need to monitor myself.

In the past I was frightened at the prospect of being rejected by women, so I tended not to give as much or not be too vulnerable for fear that I would get hurt. I think part of it was my upbringing as a male. Men don't share feelings, men don't cry, men are supposed to be strong. It's an unfortunate attribute I see in the men that I work with and it's something that I need to work on.

When I was battering, it never occurred to me that I didn't need the tough-guy image or that relationships with women could be different. Since I've made these changes in my life, my relationships with women and men have changed. When I'm with men, I'm real aware of sexist comments and attitudes. I don't want superficial relationships with people.

I'm optimistic that men who batter can change. Some of the changes are small and the process is slow, but I believe it can happen. It's been over ten years since I battered and I've been violence-free. Yet I still take an inventory of what I'm doing in my life.

Men that come into our groups in Duluth are so angry, just like I was. They're angry at the police, the courts, and their partners. I know this will sound strange, but the best thing that ever happened to me was getting arrested. I finally had to look at my behavior. I had to stop conning everyone, including myself.

The Superman Myth

These are confusing times for men. Society's expectations of men—and men's expectations of themselves—are varied and in many ways unrealistic and unhealthy. Regardless of certain positive changes that have occurred in society, men still get conflicting messages about what being a man means.

Movie star John Wayne was the quintessential tough guy male. He was big, he swaggered, he fought, and he never let his emotions get in the way. He was a cowboy, a soldier, a real man. The characters John Wayne played expected women to be submissive. In one film, he put a woman over his knee and spanked her like a child. If he showed pain, it was only in private, like a "man" does.

The modern-day John Wayne types can be found in many of the roles played by Clint Eastwood, Sylvester Stallone, Chuck Norris, and Arnold Schwarzenegger. Their characters are tough, fearless, and usually get their way. Their tough exterior is projected as attractive to the female stars, whom they usually save from a dangerous situation. These "supermen" are so courageous that they boldly fight, or kill, scores of bad guys single-handed.

While the media plays up these "superheroes" regularly, other social institutions perpetuate the superman myth as well. *"We're looking for a few good men."* This advertisement for the marines is aimed at young men who will be trained to be disciplined and unfeeling, ready to act as killing machines if ordered into combat. In our cities, boys and young men join gangs, wear colors, and are ready to kill each other at younger and younger ages. Gang members are expected to be fearless. Fighting the enemy, being willing to kill proves your loyalty and manhood. Corporations look for audacious, bold leaders to watch out for the bottom line and defeat the competition. Sports teams demand gutsy participants who, if needed, will play while injured. Men must win at any cost.

If being a man means strength and toughness, then what are you if you fail to meet these expectations? You are a failure, a sissy, or a coward. I was recently at a playground and listened to young boys as they played and roughhoused. One boy was being picked on for some reason. The others called him a faggot and a woman. Analyzing the put-down was easy. If you are not a man then you are a homosexual or, worse, a woman. This devaluing of homosexuals and women spills over into and contaminates our adult thinking and our adult lives.

Boys are taught to purge anything in themselves that society regards as feminine. I remember in junior high school being with a group of my friends at a local hangout. I crossed my legs, but not in the traditional male way of legs apart, one ankle on the other knee. One of the boys ridiculed me, saying that I was sitting like a woman. I was humiliated. After that I became very conscious of how I sat, so that I would not be considered feminine by my male peers.

Men are socialized to view so-called "feminine" characteristics—sensitivity and the expression of feelings—with hostility. These qualities are perceived as opposite to what is required to be a *real* man—or a superman. Already as boys they become afraid of their gentler feelings, of any vulnerability that will expose them to the scorn and violence of their peers. By the time they are men, they have learned to deny those feelings or have lost touch with them altogether. These negative attitudes, coupled with expectations of how men are supposed to behave in relationships, affect the way men and women relate to each other.

The superman myth dies hard, because support for this myth starts at an early age. And it affects men as well as women. As long as the myth is supported by society, both men and women will maintain unrealistic and destructive expectations in their relationships with each other.

Our socialization as boys and the impact it has on us as men is evident in an exchange that group leader MaryAnn had with one of the men in our groups. MaryAnn cofacilitated groups with me in the early eighties. She is a formerly battered woman and always brought important insights to our groups. (MaryAnn's interchanges with men in our groups appear throughout the book.)

> **MaryAnn:** Rick, you mentioned an argument that you had with your son and how your wife Sheila was angry with you because of the way you handled it. How did things finally get resolved?

> **Rick:** I'm not sure they did. She thinks I push him too hard in sports. I coach his hockey and baseball team and I can't show favorites. I push the kids, sure. But I think that discipline and drive is what it takes to win. I think it's important for boys to learn certain qualities at a young age.

> **MaryAnn:** Perhaps. Any reactions to what Rick is saying?

> **Jason:** I don't know. I remember my father screaming from the sidelines when I played football in high school. I hated it. It was like winning was so important to him. He was kind of a football star when he played in high school and he talked about his playing days all the time. Even though he thought he was helping me, you know, giving me encouragement, I just felt like a failure. I'll never forget the time I sprained my ankle in practice. I told him that I had told the coach that I didn't think I could play in the tournament game. He just looked at me with disgust and said, 'You goddamned sissy.' I'll never forget that.

From the Bible to literature to modern media, women are stereotyped as weak and overly sensitive, and male identification with so-called "female" qualities is regarded as something to be shunned. Yet, paradoxically, on an interpersonal level men may also perceive women as powerful. They often assert that women get their power through manipulation and really want to dominate men. This also translates into hostility toward women, because many men are threatened by women's power. Both in the workplace and the home, these men attempt to suppress women's power because it threatens their need for control and challenges the belief that women are to be subservient and men are to be in charge.

Today, many men are finding ways to discard the tough-guy armor and redefine what being a male is all about. This is partly a result of women's frustration with being controlled and partly men's own recognition of the emotional, spiritual, and physical destructiveness of trying to live up to the superman image. These men are not threatened by equality with women because they have found benefits they never imagined. They are beginning to enjoy intimacy in their relationships, discover their children, and live healthier lives. These men are joining women in seeking a world where both sexes are equal.

It will be easier to shed our unrealistic expectations of maleness and the negative beliefs men have about women when society as a whole begins to debunk the superman myth. As parents, we can help to dispel our childrens' false perceptions of masculinity and femininity. We can model and communicate the importance of boys and men living more complete, emotionally varied lives, rather than being trapped in the cold, controlled, one-dimensional tough-guy image which, in reality, is neither real nor healthy—nor tough.

How Our Culture Encourages Violence

How do disagreements get settled in relationships? Who makes the final decision? Who gets the last word? Many men believe that the decision must be theirs. They believe that there cannot be two bosses, and that someone has to settle conflicts about children, money, social events, and the host of other issues that fill a relationship. In order to justify taking this power, many men fall back on tradition: being the man in the house means getting to call the shots.

John related the following story during a discussion about using money as a controlling tool. He had cut up their credit cards and closed their checking account without consulting his wife, Leslie.

John: I told her I was going to do it. Man, she'll be the first to admit that she has no self-control when it comes to money. We just can't continue to get in debt the way we do, so I took some action to change things around our spending.

Michael: Don't you think that what you did is controlling? I mean, now she has no access to money without asking you.

John: It might be controlling, but someone had to put a stop to it and I knew it wouldn't be her. When we get caught up, maybe we can change.

Michael: So she gets an allowance from you.

John: I worked out a budget for food, the kids' expenses, and some basic spending money; if you want to call that an allowance, fine.

Michael: And how does Leslie feel about this?

John: She's a little pissed, but she'll get over it.

The group had a lengthy discussion about who gets to decide issues like who handles the money. Some men in the group agreed with John, believing that the man needed to take charge. Others saw it as patronizing and controlling. John saw nothing wrong with his actions.

It is difficult to say what lasting impact John's behavior will have on Leslie. She may feel powerless to challenge John and may lose self-esteem, because she is being treated like a child. She may become dependent and fearful. Or she may feel resentful and angry about his controlling behavior, and begin to lose respect for him. All of these will damage their relationship.

If John wants respect, love, and mutual trust in his relationship with Leslie, his behavior is unlikely to help him get it. Yet many men share John's belief that they should make all the decisions, even if they do not come right out and say so. Some feel it is their right, others feel it is their responsibility because, ultimately, "the man must make the hard decisions." In both cases they are responding to traditional forces in our culture.

In past generations, the roles of men and women seemed etched in stone. Social expectations were fairly clear: men were the breadwinners and women took care of house and family. In most marriage ceremonies, both civil and religious, the words "honor" and "obey" were directed at the woman and her new responsibility to her husband. Her obligations included taking care of the majority of the domestic duties: cleaning the house, cooking the meals, bearing and rearing the children, and responding to the emotional and sexual needs of her husband. Clearly, her role was to serve her husband, and this social arrangement was for a long time reflected in law.

In the book *Violence Against Wives*, researchers Rebecca and Russell Dobash note that the first Western laws relative to marriage were implemented by the Romans. These laws obliged women to conform themselves entirely to the temper of their husbands. Roman husbands were allowed to chastise, divorce, or kill their wives for engaging in certain behaviors.

Throughout medieval times, the Christian church sanctioned the beating and domination of women. The church's marriage manuals advised the subordination of women and prescribed the use of flogging so that the men could maintain appropriate moral order at home. (3)

The legal status of wives in the United States has its roots in European culture. In the United States, a husband could legally physically chastise his wife for indiscretions until the end of the nineteenth century. Although laws have recently been passed in most countries that make wife-beating illegal, the reality is that women are continually being beaten for not complying with their partners' standards and wishes.

Life is changing all around the globe, but in some cultures the status of women seems to have altered little since the Middle Ages. In certain Moslem countries, women's faces must still be covered with the traditional veil. In orthodox Jewish communities, a wife cannot get a divorce without the agreement of her husband. In India, women are still burned for not bringing a big dowry to their new family. In Brazil, men can kill their wives with impunity if they can prove sufficient jealous passion. Throughout Latin America, men are expected to have mistresses while women are ostracized for similar behavior. In Japan, thousands of predominantly Southeastern Asian women are virtually enslaved in a sex industry to serve Japanese men. In Russia, where language requiring gender equality was written into the constitution, women have been given the opportunity to work in areas typically dominated by men—but are still expected to take care of domestic tasks at home on their own.

Western Europe and North America have made impressive strides toward equality. Yet the majority of women in these societies still earn half or less of what men are paid in the workplace. There are still very, very few women in the upper echelons of government and business. And, perhaps worst of all, in the United States, 1,500 women are killed every year by their husbands and boyfriends. (4) We still have far to go.

Some men in our groups use the examples of other cultures to argue that it is perfectly acceptable for men to dominate "their" women. However, women in all cultures are challenging this position of privilege. We see emerging struggles for equality in Europe, China, Japan, countries in Africa, the Middle East, in Latin America, and among women from various cultures who reside in the United States.

If you peel back the rationalizations, most men, regardless of culture, know that devaluing and hurting women is not right. No race or gender has the right to dominate another. Any denial of this fundamental equality is sexism. We need to rethink these outdated beliefs and values that are dehumanizing to women and (though in a different way) to men as well.

Violence against women is a direct result of the sexist attitudes and beliefs which condone male domination over women. You may not see yourself as sexist, or as someone who believes in male dominance, but as a group the male gender in all its institutions has discriminated against, or sought to control, women. Violence is the cornerstone of this control.

All men benefit from male violence, whether we wish to or not. Even though I try not to participate in acts of sexism, my experiences are shaped by a sexist culture. For instance, when the sun goes down, my partner, mother, sister, and female friends cannot walk downtown or even in their own neighborhoods because they are afraid of being attacked by men. I do not experience that fear, and consequently have more mobility in the world than women.

One night, a female friend called and asked if I would walk her to the store. She was afraid because a number of sexual attacks had occurred in her neighborhood. I remember feeling somewhat powerful and even chivalrous in my traditional protective role. She had chosen me to protect her from all those other men. What was I, as a man, gaining from this situation? A feeling of personal power in relation to her and her dependence—however momentary—on me. The situation boosted my sense of traditional male power.

Violence against women will cease when men renounce the thinking and practice of dominance. We can begin to do this on an individual basis at home, at work, and in our community. When we begin to speak up, other men will listen and the seeds of change will be planted. I hope men will take the initiative and work with other men to confront sexism and violence, not to get approval from women, but because it is the right thing to do for women and men.

One way men can comprehend violence against women is to imagine the effects of sexism from a personal perspective. If you have a daughter, I am sure you want her to have every opportunity to succeed. You want her to be able to work without fear of harassment. You want her to be safe from sexual assault. If she marries, you want her husband to treat her with respect.

If you thought she was being battered, you would be outraged. Yet your daughter, like all women, faces real danger at the hands of men. She also faces obstructions every day to achieving what she can in the world, because of sexism. There are truly many reasons for men to change. These are just a few.

Every day, throughout this country, people are dying as a result of domestic abuse. From our farms to our towns and cities, people are asking: what can be done? We can begin by trying to understand how our attitudes and beliefs about women, men, and relationships ultimately influence how we treat each other. Once we understand this, we can make lasting changes.

History teaches us that societies and cultures change through experience, awareness, and knowledge. We once thought the world was flat and bloodletting cured disease. These beliefs seem foolish today. By breaking through the walls of ignorance and prejudice we *can* change longstanding beliefs. We are beginning to understand the effects of sexism and racism. We know that when one group of people dominates another they use violence and oppression to maintain their position. Hopefully, the belief that one gender, race, or religion is superior to another will one day seem as ridiculous as sacrificing humans to please the gods.

The Struggle for Equality

Living out equality, dealing with the changes it brings, raises profound issues. Men and women are unsure how to relate to each other in a world of changing societal norms. For many, their personal experiences with marriage and relationships have been confusing. Only a generation ago, few questioned the traditional arrangement of male and female roles. But in these changing times, men and women often give and get conflicting signals and messages about who they should be and how they should act and interact with each other.

Women are demanding equality in the workplace, the family, and all institutions of society. Men can support this effort, yet

many do not. Some resist the prospects of equality because they
think there are certain "natural" reasons for men to be dominant. Even those who profess to support women's liberation
sometimes experience confusion, fear, and distrust in their relationships with women. Where does this come from? What do
men fear about equality with women? Why are we so resistant?
The following discussion occurred in one of our groups.

> **Michael:** Terry, you say you believe in equality between a
> man and a woman, but that the man gets to decide when the
> two together can't.
>
> **Terry:** Yes. The Bible is clear about this, also. It basically says
> that the man should treat a wife with respect but that the wife
> should submit to the judgment of the husband.
>
> **Michael:** I would appreciate it if we could leave the Bible out
> of this discussion.
>
> **Terry:** Fine. But it's not just the Bible. Men think on a rational
> basis and the woman reacts on a more emotional basis, and
> that's just a plain fact. So it makes sense that on certain deci-
> sions, the man must make the final decision.

In the group, about half of the men agree with Terry.

> **Michael:** Well, I don't know about your relationship, Terry.
> From my experience, unless someone wants to be in a sub-
> missive position, there will always be conflict. You will be im-
> posing your will on your partner, based on your belief that you
> have the right to have power over her because of her gender.
>
> **Terry:** I'm not imposing my will, because she also believes
> that it's her role in the family.

Variations on Terry's beliefs are numerous. In order to
justify having power over someone, you must on some level
assume that there is a rational or "natural" reason for you to
have that power. Consider the following analogy.

European settlers and explorers came to the Americas about 500 years ago. They sought to exploit natural resources and claim the land for their use; however, they encountered indigenous people who had been on the continent for thousands of years. The church at that time believed all non-Christians were savages and heathens. Consequently, the explorers believed they had God on their side as they sought to take over the new land by dispossessing the indigenous people.

In order to oppress, the oppressor needs to dehumanize the person(s) he is oppressing, which is precisely what the invading Europeans did. They saw the indigenous people as defective because they did not embrace European culture and religion. So, persecution was easily justified.

Paulo Freire, a Brazilian writer and activist, wrote extensively on the effects of oppression. In his book, *Pedagogy of the Oppressed*, he explained, "The more oppressors control the oppressed (indigenous people), the more they change them into inanimate things. When the oppressed resist subjugation, they are perceived by oppressors as savages and subversives who are violent and barbaric when they react to the violence of the oppressors." (5)

Notice the parallels between the European view of indigenous people and the beliefs some men have about women. Many cultures stereotype women as being deceitful, manipulative, and weak. Several religions consider them sinful, fallen, or without spiritual merit just because of their gender. So men believe they are superior to women and use these religious or cultural stereotypes to justify their beliefs, to dehumanize women and to oppress them.

People who are oppressed usually resist their oppressors. No one likes being hurt or treated unfairly. No one likes being silenced. However, this is what a man who batters does. He robs his partner of autonomy and equality in the relationship and he imposes his will by violence and other abusive tactics.

This does not mean that all women are oppressed. Most women experience discrimination and sexism in their lives, but are not necessarily individually oppressed. In *Ain't I A Woman*, bell hooks discusses how it has been inappropriate for white women in the women's movement to compare their experiences with those of people of color. She calls attention to the fact that in the hierarchy of American society white men are at the top and white women are second. (6)

Additionally, not all women are oppressed in their relationships with men. In many relationships there is an equal distribution of power. In some relationships women may exert more control than men in the household. And clearly, women of economic means have many more options open to them than some poor men.

Regardless of class, race, and religion, however, when violence is introduced it changes everything. Violence is the weapon of those seeking power, and as long as men use violence to overpower women they will ultimately have unsatisfying relationships. They may get to call the shots, but at a great cost. Their partners will be alienated and resentful, and may turn against them. Their children will most assuredly be affected. Their sons may adopt their father's beliefs, and their daughters may see themselves as less important than males and deny their own potential.

When society changes and we are confronted with new ideas we may initially resist. We may not want to change because of fear of the unknown. However, working together with women for equality, both personally and in a broader social arena, can change men's lives for the better. They will see the benefits of strength and love in their relationships, in how their children view the world, and in their increased self-respect.

What Men Expect from Relationships

When men and women date or get married, they bring certain expectations to the relationship. And while these are changing, many men and certainly some women adhere to what we might define as a traditional relationship.

In traditional relationships, women take on the role and responsibilities of a "traditional wife." In this system, women are responsible for the majority of household and childcare responsibilities and agree to some form of submissive relationship to their husbands.

Some women say that they still find satisfaction with this arrangement. However, society does not value the traditional stay-at-home mother any more. Society sees her work in the house, including child rearing, as less important and far less prestigious than her husband's work outside the home. It is no wonder that in the last few decades women began to question and resist their traditional role, demanding something different.

To this was added the economic reality that a one-person income was no longer enough to support a large majority of American families. This led to massive changes in the United States in the 1970s and 1980s. In growing numbers, women went back to school and entered the work force to do something for themselves, something that provided a different kind of meaning in their lives, something that gave them economic independence and social freedom. These changes have not been easy for women, and men have met many of their attempts with scorn and hostility.

The following discussion about the role of men and women took place at one of our groups.

MaryAnn: We've been discussing what it means to be in a traditional relationship these past couple of weeks. Many of us grew up in that setting. Do you see any problems with this kind of relationship?

Carl: I don't think today that it's possible. It's pretty rare that your wife can stay at home and do the traditional wifely things, purely because of economics.

Bill: Yet, I feel that even though the "Father Knows Best" family isn't very commonplace, if I had the opportunity, that's what I would want.

MaryAnn: What do you mean by that?

Bill: If I had the money, I would want my wife to stay home, rather than work. Sometimes I feel like I've failed as a husband and a father because I can't make that happen.

MaryAnn: You would want your wife not to work and stay home with the children?

Bill: You bet. I don't think it's a good situation for kids to be in day care. I know this sounds old-fashioned, but I think a woman should be in the home, at least until the kids have grown.

While some men in the group did not share Bill's beliefs, others expressed confusion about what women, other men, and society expect of them. For many men, the inability to make enough money on their own creates a sense of failure. This was particularly true for men who had traditional and often rigid expectations of the roles of men and women.

You may question why I am presenting the so-called traditional relationship as outdated. Your parents may have succeeded in one. But do you really believe it is fair? Would you be happy in the "traditional wife" role?

I have heard men say they would not mind staying home during the day, sheltered from the demands of the workplace with no worries about making money. After further discussion, however, most men admit that they would feel terribly isolated and in many ways powerless if they had to rely solely on their partners for money; they would not feel equal or comfortable in the "traditional wife" role.

During one training session I attended, some people in the audience argued that a traditional relationship is fine providing both parties are in agreement and the man handles his dominant position in a benevolent manner. I countered that any time you have a relationship where one person has power over the other, you make assumptions about the value of the two parties. How many of us would be happy if our well-being and perhaps even our life depended on the "benevolence" of another? Not many.

For a long-term relationship to function in a healthy way, in fact to function at all, the stereotypical traditional inequality has to be abandoned. There are some women who share their husbands' views about the role of men and women. They espouse traditional relationships and support a man's position of authority in the home. They assert that egalitarian relationships and feminism are in conflict with traditional family values. I believe women and men who share these traditional beliefs are wary of change. They refuse to consider another way for families to exist, and they often view domestic violence as a marital problem caused by a woman not fulfilling her wifely obligations.

These attitudes are short-sighted, reactionary, and out of touch with reality. Furthermore, they contribute to the subordination of women. Men who subscribe to rigid sex roles are more inclined to justify their use of violence against a partner who is struggling for equality. When men say things like, "You've got to keep her in her place," or "She's just an uppity woman," they are echoing the traditional male expectations of the role of women, and they are exposing the roots of men's violence.

2

The Origins of Abuse and Sexual Violence

*Cassie's Story — Bernice's Story — The Violence
We Learn at Home — The Violence We Learn
From Society — Why We Use Violence —
Sexual Violence — The Impact of Violence
on Sexual Relationships*

I interviewed Cassie and Bernice about living with abusive men. Their accounts of what they experienced brings in a perspective that men often do not hear. In this section and throughout this book you will hear their stories.

Cassie's Story

My partner and I lived together for eleven years. We were both in the armed services when we met. When we got out of the service we moved to the Virgin Islands. The physical abuse started almost immediately. I was taught that you stay in a relationship no matter what, so I was determined to make the relationship work.

I left him one year because of the continued abuse and went to live with my family in Michigan. He came up there and we started to work on our issues. I moved in with him again. He wasn't violent during that year but when we'd argue he would throw stuff close to me. He'd throw an ashtray a few inches from my head, then he'd say "I didn't hit you." At the time I thought, well that's true, he didn't hit me.

We moved back to the Virgin Islands and the violence started again. After he hit me, he would say that if I just hadn't done this or said that, he wouldn't have hit me. So I stopped doing or saying things that apparently were setting him off. He told me not to yell, so I stopped yelling. He told me he wouldn't hit me if I got a job, so I got a job. He told me he wouldn't hit me if I didn't drink, so I quit drinking. But the violence didn't stop. He always had a reason. I kept trying to change my life so I wouldn't get hit.

I think the worst time was when he punched me so hard in the face that it split my head open. On another occasion he kicked me in the stomach and broke three of my ribs.

I got a restraining order against him and he left the island. I have limited contact with him today except for visitation with the children. I think he could have changed if he had gotten some education or been confronted with his behavior early on. We didn't really know what to do or where to go. We went to counseling once but the counselor didn't want to address the abuse that was going on.

I know that he knew what he was doing wasn't right. Once he introduced me to a female friend of his who was being battered. He was outraged and concerned and wanted to find ways of helping her. Ironically, he couldn't make the connection between what he was doing to me and what was happening to this woman. That's why I think if there would have been some direct intervention by a counselor or someone he might have been forced to look at his own behavior. . . .

Healing for me is a long process. I thought when I left him everything would be okay, but it wasn't. It wasn't until I started going to women's groups and sorting through everything that had happened that I started to heal. I never thought I was a battered woman. But I am gaining self-confidence. I don't know if I'll ever marry again. It's strange that after all that happened, I still have feelings for my ex-partner. I mean, we spent eleven years together and had children together. Yet I don't think I could ever go back. My trust level with men is pretty low and I'm not sure I would want to take the chance of another relationship.

Bernice's Story

I lived with my partner for three-and-half years. When we first started dating, I liked the fact that he had claimed me. It made me feel good that he found me attractive and that he wanted me. At that time, he was very supportive and bought me a lot of presents.

He was an up-and-coming public official so looks were important to him. He wanted me to dress a certain way so we looked good together. I went along with that, but he became more and more controlling. I had mixed feelings about his controlling nature, but I grew up believing that men were supposed to have the power in the household, that the man was master in his home. I believed a woman's role was to maintain a neat home, be well organized, and make good meals. I thought these domestic things were a reflection on me as a person, as a woman.

He insisted that I make the bed right after we got up in the morning. After dinner, especially if we had company over, I had to clean the dishes immediately after we ate. He would give me a certain amount of money each week and, if it wasn't enough, he made me show him the receipts. At the time none of this seemed unreasonable. Of course today, I recognize how controlling he was. I know that his expectation that a woman should be subservient was wrong.

The first time he hit me was after we got home from a political event. Some of the men were talking and putting women down. They were saying things like the only way women get ahead is by sleeping their way to the top. I got into an argument with them and my partner pulled me away and said, "Who the fuck do you think you are? Don't you ever talk that way in front of my friends again." He was upset with me because he believed what these guys were saying and he didn't want me speaking my mind and embarrassing him. All the way home he berated me, telling me I was stupid and worthless. When we got home, he slammed me up against the wall and punched me several times. And though he apologized later, he told me that he wouldn't tolerate his woman asserting herself. The violence continued and I finally told him that if it didn't stop I was leaving. He said the only way I would leave would be in a body bag. I stayed because I was afraid of him, but then I finally made the move. We were arguing about my leaving and he hit me in the face with a pop bottle and knocked out most of my teeth. He waited five or six hours before he brought me to the hospital. There I was, dazed, with my teeth hanging out and my face completely swollen, listening to this man apologize. I left after that happened.

I'm not sure this man is capable of change. I'm sure he's battering another woman today. His whole existence was having power over women. And in a strange way I think he got off on the violence.

I'll never forget how he treated me. Because of him, I see all men as a threat to me. Sadly, even my male sons are a threat, because of their size and the way boys and men are socialized. As long as men have power over women I'll be resentful. I'd like to be in a relationship at some time but it's something I can't visualize because of those experiences.

Women and Violence

Now that you've heard the stories, this is what violence is: hitting, slapping, punching, yelling; knocked-out teeth, split-open heads, broken ribs; angry stares, death threats, flying ashtrays; domination and control.

Both Bernice and Cassie were devastated by the violence they experienced. Both changed to meet their partners' demands. They adapted to survive, yet the violence continued. Finally, both women made the decision to get out.

These women were battered severely. Your violence may not have escalated to the levels described in their stories. You may even be inclined to measure your behavior against the actions of Cassie's and Bernice's ex-partners, and think that what you have done isn't as bad. It is vitally important that you remember that in both cases *the first incident was not severe.* There were apologies and promises. But in both cases the violence escalated and both men became criminally abusive.

In an attempt to understand the reality of a woman living in an abusive relationship, researchers Rebecca and Russell Dobash interviewed 109 women who had been battered. They found that the women's experiences and responses to the violence were fairly similar.

The Dobashes found that when the first assault occurs, most women think the act is an aberration, in other words, they think that the behavior is not normal. The man usually apologizes and the woman accepts his promise that he will never be violent with her again. When the second assault occurs, the level of violence increases and most women leave. They go to a parent's or a friend's home or a shelter. But the Dobashes found that when a woman leaves at this stage, her motivation is to teach her partner a lesson, not to end the relationship. If the woman believes that her partner has learned a lesson, she returns.

After the third assault, the violence escalates further and the woman usually leaves again. She may return because she does not have the financial resources to live on her own, or she fears she will lose the children, or she fears for her safety. (6)

If she stays in the relationship it is because she has to, not because she wants to. She may begin abusing alcohol or drugs to anesthetize herself because the relationship is unbearable. She may become physically or emotionally sick. Some women try to adapt. They placate their partners to lessen the chances of being hit and try their best to live with the situation. Like Cassie and Bernice, they abandon any hope of salvaging the relationship. The love they once felt evaporates, and they prepare to leave.

I advise women that they should leave after the first assault. That may sound harsh, but my experience working with men who batter is that the violence simply continues unless there is intervention.

As the Dobashes concluded in their research, women often go back because they want to believe the relationship can be saved. I ask women who go back to talk to advocates for battered women. They need to understand the dynamics of an abusive relationship. And they need to be aware that if their partners do not get help, they will usually batter again.

For this reason, a woman who does give her partner a second chance needs to develop a safety plan. A safety plan includes emergency phone numbers, people she can call for assistance, and places to stay if she senses her partner becoming abusive again. She should also insist that her partner get help—which does not mean just a couple of counseling sessions. If he is truly motivated to change, he will make a commitment to counseling or a domestic violence program. If he is willing to get help and be accountable for his behavior the relationship can heal. Only when a woman is relatively certain that her partner will not use violence again can the couple work on their problems together.

For men who are currently in a relationship and have been violent, your partner may be at the stage where she is willing to give you another chance. Make use of the opportunity: get help. However, she may be at the stage where she wants to end the relationship. This is a familiar consequence of domestic abuse. If that is the case, you cannot undo what has occurred but you can begin to make changes for yourself. You will probably enter into a new relationship at some point and you should get help now to avoid becoming abusive with a new partner.

The Violence We Learn at Home

Boys who witness domestic assaults when growing up are more likely to use violence as adults. Researchers estimate that 50–70% of men who batter either witnessed battering at home or were themselves abused by a parent. (7)

Many people believe that men learn to use violence as children. They see their fathers use violence with no negative repercussions for their actions, and they get the message that it works. (8)

Another message the child gets is that the father is boss. He gets to discipline not only his children, but also his wife. He seems omnipotent. Some times the child may sense that there is something wrong with the behavior, at other times he may conclude that his father had a rational reason for becoming so angry and abusive.

Either way, the messages etched in the minds of children who observe violence are indelible. Men in our groups have said that they had vowed not to repeat the domestic abuse they saw as children. However, for most of them, when conflicts arose with their partners and they felt they could not win or control the situation, a light from the past would signal: "hit her." With a hit or a punch they could change the situation, just like their fathers did. And if there are no consequences for the violence, i.e., getting arrested or losing the relationship, the behavior becomes reinforced.

Many men have had childhood experiences that were not happy. Some were abused or mistreated by parents and others watched their fathers abuse their mothers. Some men did not experience physical violence but were verbally abused or got little emotional support at home.

Even if you had a terrible childhood, it is important that you not blame your past for your actions today. For one thing, holding onto painful childhood and adult experiences only aggravates an unhealed wound. Secondly, regardless of how and where you learned about violence, you must address your *current* way of reacting to women in relationships, because that is something you can change. Remember: men make a *personal* choice to become violent regardless of what they have been exposed to during their childhood.

Barbara Hart, an attorney who has written extensively on domestic violence, states, "Perhaps growing up in a culture of violence and in a family marked by violence desensitizes people to violence or makes it harder for them to choose lives free of violence. But what has been learned can be unlearned and relearned." (9)

Exercise: Learning About Violence

In order to understand some of the reasons for violence in your life, walk through your personal history and examine your past experiences. Some of those experiences still affect you today, and reliving them may make you feel uncomfortable. In the following exercises you can either write down your responses in a journal or notebook, or remember your responses as you go through each step.

STEP ONE: Find a comfortable chair, relax, and close your eyes. Think back to the first time you witnessed someone being physically hurt by another person. This scene doesn't necessarily have to be one that took place in your childhood. Some examples might be: one parent assaulting another parent, a parent beating your sister or brother, a bully abusing a friend or schoolmate.

Try to recall the incident in detail. What was your reaction to the violence? How did you feel? Did you talk to anyone about what you saw or how you felt?

_____

_____

_____

MaryAnn had the following discussion about the impact of witnessing violence in one of our groups. She asked Reggie about how he felt when he saw his father beating his brother for stealing a car.

Reggie: I was horrified. I'd never seen anyone get punched like that close up except on T.V. I remember my brother covering up his head to shield himself from the blows. I felt totally powerless to do anything. I realized that he probably deserved to be punished for stealing the car but even at my young age that beating seemed severe.

MaryAnn: Were you surprised by the fury of your father's anger?

Reggie: I was definitely surprised by his anger and his actions. I'm not sure what the lasting impact was on me, except maybe the experience made me conscious about never getting so angry at my children where I could resort to violence like my father did that night.

STEP TWO: Think of a time you were the victim of abuse or violence as a child or adult. If you have never been a victim of abuse or violence, describe a situation where someone was abusive or violent in a manner that felt intimidating.

What was your reaction to being the victim? How did you feel after the incident? Did you talk to anyone about what happened?

_____

_____

_____

In one of our groups, MaryAnn had the following discussion with Roland about being a victim of violence.

MaryAnn: You said you felt powerless during the mugging. Do you really think that you had any other option?

Roland: I think most men fantasize that they could do something heroic. My fantasy is that I had a black belt in karate. I can visualize my hits and kicks as I take these two guys down. Just like in the movies.

MaryAnn: So because you couldn't be like Clint Eastwood you saw yourself as a failure?

Roland: In part because my wife was there, I felt like less of a man.

MaryAnn: How did your wife react to you after the incident?

Roland: Well, both she and the police kept emphasizing that we had no other options, but I *still* wish I would have done something. It's amazing how we men are socialized about violence. I think that most of us are horrified when we are confronted with it, but feel that somehow we should be able to stand up to any challenge.

MaryAnn: Does that experience affect you today?

Roland: Sure. I think about it and my inaction a lot. I'm nervous walking in certain parts of town. If I see more than one man coming toward me I start to prepare. I'm much more sensitive to the psychological impact of violent crime on victims.

STEP THREE: Recall a time when you used violence against someone. Think of an adult experience that really had an impact on you. If you have not used violence, think of a time you used intimidation against a past or present partner or your children. If neither applies, think about a childhood experience.

What was your reaction to your own violent act? Did anyone confront you about your behavior? If yes, how did you respond to their questioning? Did you make excuses, blame the other person, or admit what you had done?

In one of my groups, we discussed the use of violence.

T.J.: I remember slapping my daughter Elisha hard. I couldn't believe I did it. She was in shock and the look she gave me was one of total disbelief, almost betrayal. She ran from the room screaming.

Michael: How did she respond to you afterward?

T.J.: She was actually concerned about how upset I was. I apologized and promised her that I would never allow my anger to get to that point again.

Michael: Do you think that slap changed things?

T.J.: Well, I think that some of the innocence of our father-daughter relationship changed. I also became very aware of my temper and my ability to be violent. We've had many arguments since, but I'm very conscious of what I'm capable of because of that incident.

STEP FOUR: Review step three, when you recalled being violent to someone. Imagine the same situation occurring today. How would you respond now? Would you handle the situation differently? What are the alternatives to using violence or intimidation in that situation? (9)

_____

_____

_____

The purpose of this and other exercises in this book is to learn from our past experiences and our mistakes. Much has happened in our lives to shape who we are, yet each of us has the strength and capacity to change. We can live our lives differently by learning from the past.

The Violence We Learn from Society

Many men who choose to use violence did not grow up in households where their fathers hit their mothers. In a society where negative attitudes and violence toward women are commonplace, boys and men may experiment with behaviors that conflict with the values they learned in the home.

Our attitudes about women, men, and relationships can be traced to many childhood experiences. Our characters are developed by what we learn and observe in school, church, neighborhoods, and our families of origin. Our experiences become a blueprint for living, a foundation for how we respond to situations throughout our lives.

Boys learn a great deal of violence from the culture in which they live. Boys play imaginary games of war, compete in violent sports, read violent comic books, watch violent movies, and are exposed to violent pornography. Boys are taught at an early age that violence is an acceptable way to handle conflict. If they refrain from using violence they may be ridiculed by other boys. When this occurs, they feel that they do not measure up as "men."

In Chapter 5 you will meet Mark. He explained that when he was growing up his father treated his mother with respect. He rarely heard an argument, and saw no violence between them. In school, though, his male friends had a strong influence on him and he began putting girls down to become accepted within a certain group. Like his friends, he wanted to be in charge when dating. And like his friends, he learned that slapping a girl was something a boy was entitled to if his girlfriend flirted with another boy, ignored him, or talked back. Using violence against women was not something Mark learned at home. He developed these attitudes among his peers, and got reinforcement for his behavior from his male friends.

The following discussion in one of my groups focused on what influenced our beliefs about violence and women.

Lewis: You know, it's strange. Seeing my father kick the hell out of my mother all those years and the way he treated us kids, I promised myself that when I became an adult I would never be that way to my wife or kids. And here I am in this damn group.

Phil: I guess it's something that we just learn.

Michael: Are you saying that if you see and experience this stuff as children, then you automatically become abusive?

Phil: No, but this is what I apparently learned from my childhood. I used to think that my dad hitting my mom was somewhat justified, because I could tell what would set him off and I couldn't understand why she couldn't.

Randy: My father was never violent with my mother. In fact, all I saw was the two of them being very affectionate.

Michael: So Randy, you didn't observe violence in the home, yet you battered your wife. Phil just said that he thought he learned violence from watching his dad. Why do you think you started to be violent with women? Where do you think you got your messages about women and relationships?

Randy: I suppose just living. Some of my friends in high school would talk about slapping their girlfriends if they got out of line and everyone would laugh. My friends meant a lot to me and they had a lot of influence over decisions I made. When I played on the football team, I started developing this tough-guy image because I thought it would impress people. Getting into fights and slapping up your girlfriend was all just part of it.

Why We Use Violence

Violence produces immediate results—it works. Except in cases of real self-defense, I never met a man who battered who would dispute the fact that his motive was to stop his partner from saying or doing something of which he disapproved, or to punish her for doing something he did not like.

To see if this explanation fits for you, do the following exercise. It is a variation on an exercise I designed together with Ellen Pence of the Duluth Domestic Abuse Intervention Project. (10)

Exercise: Why We Use Violence

You can do this exercise by yourself or in a group. It involves recalling an incident in which you used violence toward a partner and you might want to record your thoughts and feelings in a notebook or journal. If you have not been violent, think of a time when your behavior was intimidating, i.e., you screamed, pounded your fist on a table, hit a wall, glared, or threw something at or close to someone.

Violent Incident: Think about the most recent episode in which you used violence, threats, or intimidation against a past or present partner. Choose an incident that stands out in your mind. Describe what happened and what you did.

_____

_____

_____

_____

Purpose: Describe why you were violent at that time. What did you want to have happen?

_____

_____

_____

_____

Short- and Long-term Impact: What was the short- and long-term impact of the violence on your partner, you, and the relationship?

Short-term Impact

_____

_____

_____

Long-term Impact

_____

_____

_____

Reread your answer in the purpose section. Your purpose probably was to gain something very specific, like stopping an argument or getting your way.

Now look at the impact sections. You will probably notice two things. First, in the short term you most likely got what you wanted, at least initially. Your partner may have stopped arguing, not gone out, or altered her behavior.

In the long term, however, what probably happened is the exact opposite of what you wanted. Your partner may have become distant, and intimacy between you may have been diminished. She probably became furious with you for your behavior and may have contemplated leaving the relationship.

Does this coincide with your experience?

To complete this exercise, close your eyes and relax. Review the incident you just described above. Imagine a way you could have handled the situation differently, without being violent. You may have been justifiably angry or hurt by something your partner did but, after reflection, could you have responded to the conflict without being violent?

For some men, participating in a counseling group can be helpful in understanding how growing up male in this culture has influenced their beliefs about women and relationships. For others, especially those who grew up in violent households, seeing a counselor or a therapist may be needed to unravel some of the past and finally say good-bye to it. Regardless of how you got here, though, you alone are responsible for what you do now. It is helpful—sometimes even necessary—to understand your past, but it is completely up to you to take charge of your future.

Sexual Violence

Although it has only made headlines in the last few years, sexual abuse is not a new phenomenon. Strangers and family members have molested and raped girls and women for centuries. In times of war, invading soldiers rape defenseless women as part of their conquest. Few countries and cultures have been immune to these crimes.

In some countries, if a woman reports a rape her husband and family may stone or ostracize her. Many girls and women in the U.S. do not report rape because they fear they will not be believed or will suffer the anguish of a public trial and media exposure.

The effects of being sexually abused are varied. Most survivors feel violated and are often full of rage. Some experience guilt because they were not able to stop the assault from occurring. Some survivors have difficulty trusting others or develop sexual problems. Some survivors heal quickly, for others the psychological effects of the trauma last for a long time.

Males are also the victims of sexual abuse but in far lesser numbers than females. Some men have been sexually abused by women, but most are abused by men and other boys. However, the short- and long-term effects on males who have been sexually violated are generally parallel to the effects on females.

In the following analysis, I will refer to the predominant dynamic of sexual abuse, male upon female. Research indicates that 50% of women who have been battered have also experienced sexual abuse at the hands of their partners. Sexual abuse is common in many marriages. Most men believe that sexual access is their contractual right after marriage, and many men in relationships who force or coerce their partners into having sex view their behavior as normal. Many women do not define forced acts of intercourse in a marriage or long-term relationship as rape because of confusion about perceived marital or relationship obligations.

What is the intent of sexual abuse? While sexual desire is a part of the act of rape, the principal factors are violence and domination, which make the perpetrator feel powerful. He has *conquered* this girl or woman. Boys are socialized to believe that they should initiate or pursue sex aggressively. Often they learn about sex by being exposed to pornography, which "objectifies" women by presenting them as bodies, not as persons with feelings. All this results in convoluted messages about what girls and women want and what boys and men are supposed to do. When combined with the ignorance and fear of rejection surrounding sex this creates an unstable, unfortunately often violent mixture.

Aggressive and even abusive male sexual behavior is sometimes excused as an inherent uncontrollable biological urge. In this view men supposedly have a sexual appetite that is dictated by testosterone, so their need for sex "must" be satisfied. This argument, however, is simply another excuse for objectification and dominance.

The language many men use reflects these common, exploitative sexual attitudes to women. "Hitting" on women, "scoring," and "getting laid" are terms that have little to do with love, intimacy, or even acknowledging another person, and much more with sexual conquest. With this language men are reducing women to objects, to be obtained and used.

It is a rare human being who has not been affected by societal messages about sex. Human sexuality gets categorized into right and wrong, proper or dirty. We grow up with guilt, confusion, and anxiety about sex and have few outlets to talk frankly and ask questions about our feelings and experiences.

As adults, we often do not—and cannot—communicate about sex with our partners.

In one of my groups, I read the following scenario: a man takes a female friend out to dinner. He pays for the dinner and then they go dancing and have several drinks. She invites him into her apartment. When he attempts to have sex with her she refuses and resists. He pursues her and forcefully has intercourse with her. When I asked the group whether they thought that the man had raped the woman, many said no.

Several men in the group believed there is an expectation that men are entitled to sex, given certain conditions. If a man buys a woman (his date) something, if she dresses a certain way, if they have been drinking, or if she is demonstrative, he is right in believing that she wants sex even though she says she does not. If she resists or says no, he may not believe her or may not care.

I then read another scenario in which a man pressures his wife to have sex. He tells her that it is her duty and that if she does not have sex with him, he will "get it" elsewhere. She submits. Again, many of the men in the group did not see any problem with this kind of pressure.

Certainly many women desire sex from men. For better or for worse there are certain games that both sexes play. However, if we look at sexuality as it has been defined by and for men in our culture, issues of violence and exploitation are inescapable. Rape, buying of sex (prostitution), and producing and using hard-core pornography depersonalize women and destroy lives. When we read studies indicating a high percentage of men would rape if they could get away with it, we have to question the whole male orientation of sexuality and its relationship to domination and violence.

The success of the recent film *Indecent Proposal*, and the phenomenon of popular polls that followed it asking whether men would let their partners sleep with another man for a million dollars, was an interesting demonstration of our confused values and ideas about sexuality, women as objects, women as male property, and the pervasive fantasy links between money and sex.

Sexual abuse is not limited to coerced sex. One women told me how her husband would consistently make derogatory comments about her body, particularly about the size of her breasts. Sometimes he would make these statements in public or in front of their children, despite the humiliation it caused her.

Another women related how her husband would bring home hard-core pornographic videos. He would make her watch the films and copy what they viewed. Many of the sexual acts were violent or painful, yet she felt she had to submit.

As men, we can untangle the negative cultural messages that all males have been exposed to about sexuality. We can speak up when media, friends, and coworkers trivialize sexual abuse through comments and jokes. When Indiana basketball coach Bobby Knight made the comment that if a woman is raped, she might as well lie back and enjoy it, there was a firestorm of criticism. Women reacted in outrage, but men were relatively silent. They either saw it as a harmless joke or were afraid that they would be seen as unmanly if they criticized the remark.

Martin Luther King, Jr. said, "A time comes when silence is betrayal." I believe that men betray their wives, sisters, mothers, and humanity by their silence.

It does not have to be this way. Men can refuse to participate in the sexual objectification of women. We can teach our sons not to use women, and to understand the importance of sexual respect in relationships. In your current or future relationship, your sexuality can be based on mutuality and respect for each other's needs.

The Impact of Violence on Sexual Relationships

My discussions with men who have battered and women who have been battered show that the sexual relationship usually changes after violence occurs. Intercourse after a violent episode is common. A man often believes that if he is sexual after being violent, his partner will see how sorry he is or how much he really loves her and will forgive him for the violence. He may believe that the tenderness that he expresses makes amends for his abuse. For some men, the violence also provides an erotic charge.

For many women, having sex after an assault can be a way of calming down a partner, and women will often submit out of fear of further violence. The experience, however, is often degrading and devoid of tender or intimate feelings. Other women are confused by sexual expression following a violent episode. They hope for the relationship to be made right. They want to be intimate and feel loved.

As Bernice explains, her sexual relationship with her partner was a mixture of violence and confusion.

> "To me, it's the ultimate in control when a man has sex with you after he has beaten you. I think my partner had this strange way of equating sex with negative attitudes about women, basically that a woman's function was for the sexual pleasure of men. It was all very confusing for me. Here this man beats me and then he's making love to me.
>
> "My partner raped me many times although I'm not sure he saw it that way. Sometimes when he had friends over he would make derogatory sexual comments about me. I felt humiliated and violated.
>
> "When we were making love and I responded in a certain way to a position that we were in, he would become abusive and beat the hell out of me. He would accuse me of sleeping around and practicing these positions because of the way I responded. This was especially traumatizing; to get beat right after making love.
>
> "Since I left my partner, I've not been sexual. I was dating this one guy and the issue of sex came up and these old memories came up and I got frightened. That part of me has really been damaged."

Cassie also experienced sexual abuse throughout her marriage, especially after a violent episode.

"I learned very early that I had no options. Sometimes he would force himself on me. I told him that I wasn't going to respond sexually but he didn't seem to care. That really reinforced this whole thing that he didn't care how he was getting sex. It didn't matter to him if I participated or not. It was the ultimate in objectification.

"I either had sex or I got beat up. I never saw it as sexual abuse at the time. Whenever we had a fight, it was never completely over until we had sex. Even when I was feeling rotten I had to submit, and for him everything was supposedly okay."

For both Bernice and Cassie the sexual abuse they experienced has stayed with them years after their relationships ended. They have been robbed of something precious: the ability to trust another human being in intimate, loving contact.

If you are still with someone whom you have abused, it is important that you listen to your partner's concerns and respect what she needs. She may feel distant or may not feel like engaging in sex because of what has gone on in the past. If she needs time, honor her request *without* making her feel guilty or pressuring her in any way. These can be confusing times for her and wounds can take a long time to heal. Guilt or pressure will only reinforce her pain and distrust.

Practitioners who work in this field unfortunately underestimate the degree to which sexual violence occurs in relationships. Women as well as men are often reticent to discuss sexual abuse when describing what has transpired in their relationships. They may also have trouble identifying certain behavior as sexual abuse.

For instance, a woman may describe an incident where she submitted to sex when she wasn't interested. She may not see her partner's pressure as coercion, and may not present it as such. A practitioner who fails to understand abusive patterns of behavior may misinterpret the level of sexual abuse in a relationship. Similarly, a man may report viewing a lot of pornographic material. He may claim it has no effect on his partner or on the relationship, but the practitioner should be skeptical of these assertions and probe for further information on the impact of pornography on the relationship.

In summary, not all men who batter are sexually abusive, but there is a higher probability that they will be. We need to address this issue squarely. Men cannot assume that marriage provides a license to sexual access. Acknowledging sexual abuse in counseling or with a partner may produce shame or guilt but, like all the aspects of accountability discussed in this book, it is a part of taking full responsibility for your violence. It is a necessary step on your road toward making real changes in your life.

3

It's More Than Just Physical Violence

Jim's Story — Using Intimidation to Control —
Using Threats — Blocking Her Freedom To Decide —
Using the Children to Get to Her —
The Pain of Emotional Abuse — Understanding
and Stopping Battering

The word *battering* refers to the systematic use of abusive behaviors, including physical violence, to establish and maintain control over another person. Ending your use of physical violence is the first step in your process of change. But you must also commit to ending other abusive behaviors.

Jim's Story

Jim grew up in a middle-class neighborhood in a small community in California and moved to Minnesota in his twenties. He was arrested for domestic assault and was ordered to attend our program. He was 34 at the time of this interview and had been married three times. In his story, Jim describes the very brutal violence he used in his relationships. He also discusses how he used other abusive behaviors to intimidate and control his partners.

I came from a very violent home. One night, my dad was really drunk and he was trying to force himself into the house. I knew that he would either do something to my mother or she would do something to him. The next thing I knew they were fighting outside the doorway of our apartment. He was beating on her and she grabbed a knife and stabbed him in the side and pushed him down the stairs. My father lived but the relationship didn't.

There were many times when I hid under a table to avoid the violence around me. I was always afraid because I was constantly witnessing my father and mother hurting each other. It's strange, because as a kid it all seemed kind of normal to me. I thought all families were like mine. When I started assaulting women, I never correlated my action to my upbringing, but I think now that it must have had an impact.

My stepfather also battered my mother. He punched her in the mouth, pulled her down, and kicked her when she was on the floor. I would try to stop him, but I would get thrown aside. Sometimes when I would intervene, it would slow the fight down, so every time they got into a fight, I'd try and stop it. I remember many times I would be upstairs and I would be listening to their fights for hours. I would take the pillow and cover my head and cry for the longest time. I really was afraid that they would kill each other.

My stepfather would discipline us kids with a belt that had studs on it. I remember actually feeling the welts on my rear end. Many times, my parents would go to a bar and leave us in the car while they went in to drink. In the winter we would be freezing. My brother would go into the bar and tell our parents we were cold and then they would finally come out. If we said anything in the car my stepfather hit us.

My mother was also abusive to us. When I was a teenager, I had come home late and as I rode my motorcycle into the driveway, my mother hit me on the back with a broom handle. I fell off the bike and she began hitting me on the head and on the back with this broom handle. At the time I didn't see this as abusive, because all the violence in our home seemed normal.

All through my childhood, I was very rough. I would beat up on my younger brother and my older brother would beat up on me. One time in the seventh grade I got into a fight with a kid at school. I remember being scared of him because he was kind of a bully, but I couldn't back down. When we fought I smashed his face into the brick wall of the school. I remember feeling very powerful, especially with all the kids around me saying how great I was. Also, to have beaten up this kid who I perceived to be so tough felt good.

I was violent with girls from the time I started dating. My first steady girlfriend was Terri. Once, we were at a party and everyone was drinking. I wanted her to drink and have fun, but she didn't want to. We got into an argument in the car and I grabbed her by the throat and pushed her up against the door and told her she was going to do what I wanted her to do. When I let go of her, she slapped me. I slapped her back especially hard and got into a total rage. I punched the window and broke it and left her crying in the car.

The messages that I got growing up were that women should be submissive to men. The man had total say. I believed that if women crossed the line, you had to put them in their place. I grew up believing that women were to be used and so that's what I did.

I was 19 when I met Cathy. She was 17. I had just entered the armed services. I didn't hit her until after we got married. After I had that marriage license, things changed. I felt like I owned her. After we were divorced she told me that when we were living together I treated her like a queen, but as soon as we got married, I changed. I guess I felt, prior to marriage, that I could lose her, but once I had that piece of paper, she was mine.

Of all the women that I physically abused, she got the worst of it. I can remember having parties and getting extremely intoxicated. I would get into an argument with her, throw her around, and punch her in the face. She cooked, cleaned, and took care of the children. When I wanted sex, we had it and there was to be no flak about it. In some ways I'm surprised she stayed as long as she did.

One time when she was three months pregnant with my daughter, she went to a high-school football game. She wasn't home when I thought she would be. I was in a total red rage and went looking for her. I came home and she was there. She was scared when she saw how mad I was and tried to leave. She screamed, "I'm not going to get beat up by you again!" I grabbed her and threw her 15 feet; she landed on the couch. I went over to the couch and put my left hand on her throat and began back-handing her with my other hand numerous times. She lay on the couch crying and bleeding. Even though I felt bad for what I had done to her, I thought she had brought it on herself. I was convinced that she was out looking for another guy. The way I saw it, she shouldn't have been gone so long and she should have been home with me, case closed. I really believed she asked for it.

Some years later I was up for a promotion at my job. Cathy had prepared a big meal that night with candles and everything because she knew we would find out about the promotion that day. She was all positive and in a real good mood. Well, I didn't get the promotion and was in a terrible mood when I got home. I took it out on her. I was mad because she had this meal all fixed up. I started yelling and screaming and then I threw the dinner off the table.

When I beat her I'd feel very powerful. When I would see the terror in her eyes, I knew I had won. Sometimes, though, I would feel guilty. I would tell her how ashamed I was for what I was doing, that I would get help for my drinking and I would apologize. I would usually want to have sex after my violence, and she would agree. I thought it was because she loved me, but I think now she agreed to sex to pacify me.

Our neighbors out in California used to call me "the green-eyed monster," because I was always exploding in a jealous rage. Cathy is a very pretty woman and I felt that she got a kick out of men eying the way she walked. I thought she flaunted her beauty and her body. I felt since she hurt me by making me jealous, I would hurt her by being violent.

We were having a party one night and I became jealous of a

male friend of ours who was talking with Cathy. I had been drinking a lot and was doing a lot of PCP. I started to slap her up. I made a big scene and told everyone to leave. That night, I destroyed the apartment. She left me after that incident.

Eight years after Cathy left me I was still hanging on to the relationship. I would call her, write her, and go to the town where she was living and try to see her. I would beg her to take me back. One time, I got very high on PCP, put a gun to my head and told her I would kill myself unless she took me back. I would tell Cathy that our daughter needed a father in her life. I tried everything but she was through with me.

I married Gretchen two years later, after a very short courtship. We moved to Duluth and remained married for seven years. My violence toward her was mostly grabbing her by the arms and pushing her down. I think I only hit her once. I really didn't have to be very violent with her, because she was submissive and I could make her afraid by just yelling at her. I would give her a certain look and she knew I was upset. In that marriage, I was the ultimate ruler. I don't believe that I was ever in love with her, but I stayed with her because it was convenient.

One time, I came home really drunk and demanded that she make me a steak. I went into the kitchen and there were all these dirty dishes in the sink and I flew into a rage. I started throwing the dishes at her and then I hit her in the face with the back of my hand. I started breaking everything in the house. It was Christmas time and I smashed all the presents. The kids were watching this. I threw the Christmas tree through the window. Our neighbor called the sheriff and they brought me to the detox center for drunks.

Toward the end of this relationship, Gretchen and I got into an argument about who was getting custody of our child. I punched her several times in the face. She tried to leave but I was determined not to let her take our daughter. Gretchen called the police. I attacked the police officers and was charged with assault. The court ordered me into outpatient treatment for my alcoholism and the Domestic Abuse Intervention Project in Duluth for my violence.

While in treatment I continued to drink. When I went into the Domestic Abuse Intervention Project, I was in total denial. I didn't feel I needed any help and was very angry that the court had ordered me to counseling. But after several weeks, something touched me in the group and I realized that I had a problem. The program was helpful for me because I heard the other men's stories and realized I wasn't alone. I started to see that the abuse was really wrong and that it was my responsibility to change. After completing the program and probation, I stayed on as a volunteer.

In my current relationship with Toni, things are dramatically different. When there are problems now, we sit down and talk about things and I explain how I feel. When we have conflicts today, I'm able to express my feelings and, perhaps more importantly, I listen to Toni rather then just flying off the handle. I still take time-outs. When I have visitation with my children from my past marriages, they don't see the anger and the abuse that they used to. I know they see the difference.

When I think back, I know I was dependent on women, emotionally, financially, and sexually. I felt like I needed a female partner in my life to make me whole. I had very low self-esteem and a lack of love for myself. I'm not jealous with Toni like I was in past relationships. I'm more secure with myself.

I'm proud of where I'm at today, because I made the changes to stop drinking and stop the violence. I hope that in my family the abuse stops here. My parents never recognized the abuse. I got the help I needed because I got arrested and because I went through the programs. I'm dedicating myself to being a positive role model for my children and for other men.

I call myself a recovering abuser. I do a similar thing like the 12-step program for alcoholics. I try to do positive things in my life, analyzing myself when I need to and associating with positive people. You have to get to know yourself and love yourself and then you can love others.

Using Intimidation to Control

Many men use physical violence infrequently but abuse women by resorting to other overt and covert behaviors, including intimidation. They learn how to intimidate women, other men, and their children. Some use their body language. They glare, tower over their partners, or block their physical space. Some men slam down their fists, punch walls or doors, and throw things. Intimidating behavior is frightening; the person being intimidated is never sure if physical violence will follow.

Andy, who told his story in Chapter 1, said, "If we were at a party and my partner was talking to another man, I would just look at her and she would be at my side. No one knew what was going on. It was just a look or a crooked smile and she knew."

As Bernice explains, intimidation brings immediate fear.

"When my partner was angry at me, he would walk around me while he was talking or yelling so I never knew what to expect. I'd try to maintain eye contact with him because he had hit me in the back of the head before. He wouldn't necessarily have to be talking angrily but the fact that I had to turn around and watch him was very intimidating. He knew exactly what he was doing."

Getting what you want through intimidation or simply venting your anger in the house may be temporarily satisfying for you. You may get what you want at the time. However, if people you say you love are afraid of you, how can intimacy, trust, and caring exist? Because you have behaved like this for a long time you may be oblivious to your family's fear, but I assure you, your partner and your children are afraid.

In one of my groups, George was coming to terms with his past intimidating behavior. He did not want his family to be afraid of him. He acknowledged that his abuse affected his family, and he wanted to change.

George: Ever since I started coming to this group, I'm really becoming aware of how much fear I instilled in Holly and the kids. It doesn't feel very good to know that they're still afraid of me.

Michael: That fear may be there for a while and you're going to have to be patient. You can't expect them just to forget what happened.

George: I know. But it bothers me. I can tell when I walk in the door that things change. I don't want them to be afraid of me anymore.

Michael: George, what are you like when you come home? Are you smiling and cheerful or angry and tense?

George: Well, I'm usually pretty tired. I have a stressful job and it takes a while for me to unwind. I wouldn't say that I'm overly cheerful but I'm not always angry, either.

Michael: Well, when you're feeling a certain way, sometimes your body language projects that emotion. So if you're tense, your body language may project a message like "Stay *away* from me!" What do you think?

George: Well, it's certainly possible.

Michael: Are you willing to try something?

George: Sure.

Michael: For the next week, I want you to practice the following exercise. When you get home, take a 45 minute walk before you go into the house. As you walk, think positively about yourself and your life. Put the day out of your mind. Every time something from work enters your mind, push it out, and focus on something pleasant and enjoyable. Take deep breaths when you walk and try to relax. When you enter the house, be positive.

The next week, George reported to the group that he noticed a change. People in the house seemed less anxious. George was really surprised that after only one week of doing things like taking a walk, using positive self-talk, and making an effort to change his demeanor, he achieved so many positive results.

Men who use intimidation, whether deliberately or not, need to become aware of how they respond to conflicts and problems that arise in the home. Self-monitoring and feedback from others may be necessary. If you are upset or in a bad mood, let your partner and children know that your mood has nothing to do with them. For example, you can calmly say, "I'm in a bad mood, it has nothing to do with you, and I need some time to be alone."

Sometimes men are not aware, or *choose* not to be aware, of how scary and intimidating they can be when they are angry. In a relationship where there has been no abuse, anger is not so frightening. But partners and children who have been abused have vivid memories of violence, and anger will elicit fear in them even if violence does not follow.

Sometimes men in our groups will say that punching a wall or door is better than hitting their partners. This is true. But punching an inanimate object in your partner's presence can produce the same results as hitting her, which is why intimidating behavior may be considered domestic assault in a court of law. A punched wall or a thrown object may give your partner the impression that she is next.

Men can use their voices to terrify and abuse. One woman told me that her partner's voice was like a slap across the face. A common way that men intimidate is by shouting. Some get right into their partner's face and yell. The purpose is obvious: most people are unnerved by it. If you are serious about changing, this kind of intimidation must stop. Monitor yourself by making a commitment not to shout, and to lower your voice during times of conflict.

If you are angry or upset, find another outlet to deal with your emotions. Talk with a friend, walk away from the situation that is upsetting you (see Chapter 5 on time-outs), and practice restraint. All of the men I interviewed for this book said that they continue to take time-outs when they are angry. They also said they consistently need to monitor themselves. They have learned the importance of responding to conflict in a non-intimidating manner and they do what it takes to be nonviolent.

Using Threats

Sometimes men who batter threaten further violence. Women who have been beaten in the past obviously take these threats seriously. Several men in our groups say that their partners know they would not actually do what they threatened to do. But how can their partners be sure? And if the men have been violent in the past, why wouldn't their partners think that the threats were real? Why did the men make threats in the first place?

Threats are used to elicit a response or to get your way. Whether you intend to carry out the threat or not, your partner has a reason to be afraid. Threats are a form of violence.

Some men threaten that they will take away or gain custody of the children. They know that this is an area where women feel particularly vulnerable, and they choose to exploit this vulnerability. Other men threaten to harm themselves. In one of our groups, Al discussed his threat to commit suicide.

Al: I don't know why Beverly put that stuff about me wanting to commit suicide in the court affidavit. She knows I would never do something like that.

Michael: How would she know that for sure?

Al: She knows.

Michael: In the statement, it said that you took the gun from the basement, went upstairs, and told her that you were going to kill yourself, and then you left. Why would you make those threats?

Al: Well, she had been real cold to me after I hit her, you know, real unforgiving. I thought maybe the threat of losing me

would shake her up a little and things would change. It was a
stupid thing to do, but she knew I'd never really kill myself.

Many men threaten suicide, usually when they think that
they are losing the relationship. They believe the threat of
suicide will get their partners to rethink their decision and stay.
But destructive relationships are rarely saved by threats, and
their efforts may only prolong and intensify the breakup.

A note to women: You *should* take all threats seriously. If your
partner is threatening you in any way, get advice from a battered
women's program in your area. You may need to use the legal
system or find a shelter to protect yourself. A man who is threatening violence or suicide or threatening to take the children is
dangerous and his behavior is illegal.

Blocking Her Freedom to Decide

In battering relationships, men often attempt to isolate their
partners. Either through sabotage, manipulation, or demand,
men curtail women's relationships with particular friends or
family members. Typically, men who batter either demand an
end to certain relationships or put up obstacles which make it
difficult for their partners to associate with people the men do
not like. If their partners resist their demands, their behavior
often escalates into violence.

In Bernice's case, her partner cut off her relationships with
friends for a specific reason:

"When we first started dating, I had a lot of friends and
my partner seemed okay with that. But things changed, especially when the physical violence intensified. He started to
devalue my friends. If a friend of mine gave me clothing as a
Christmas present, he would use it as a rag to wash the car. He'd
say, 'I don't know why you want to hang around her, she ain't
no good.'

"He wanted the power to make me feel bad and to make

me feel good. So my having friendships was a threat. He feared them because they could make me feel better and he wanted that exclusively."

For Cassie, her partner wanted her to better herself, but only up to a point.

"My partner encouraged me to go back to school and I did. But as I got close to graduating from college, he made things very difficult. I don't think he ever thought I'd get to that point, so when I did he said I was neglecting the house and the kids. It was literally a fight for me to get out the door to attend my classes.

"After I graduated, he encouraged me to get a job. He'd say, 'You're a smart woman, you've got a degree, and you can get a good job.' So I got a job, but I had to start at the bottom. Everything was okay and he was supportive until I started to work my way up the ladder. He got real threatened by the people that I worked with. And I think he felt inadequate because I was making more money than him. That's when the beatings started getting real bad. I think he felt less of a man."

Why does a man who batters try to inhibit his partner's relationships with others? Here are three reasons.

First, he may be afraid that his partner's friends or family members will give her information or support that will help her get out of the abusive relationship. He is usually aware of the pain he is causing and knows that the abuse will make her think about leaving. He identifies her friends as a bad influence because he suspects them of plotting with his partner to help her leave the situation.

Second, he may be, and often is, very jealous of others—especially other men. If his partner goes out with friends, he fears that she is seeking the company of another man. He is insecure, and because of the way he has treated her in the past, his insecurity about the relationship increases. He asks himself, "Why would she want to stay with me after the way I have treated her?" He is also particularly suspicious of divorced or single women because they are independent and he fears that they will give his partner ideas about leaving.

Third, he may believe that his partner does not need friends and needs only limited contact with her family. "Anything she needs emotionally or intellectually she can get from me," he thinks. He wants her world to revolve around him, and by keeping her isolated he encourages her dependence on him.

In one of our groups, we discussed isolating behavior and some of the beliefs and expectations men have when they enter a relationship.

Michael: Allen, you were talking last week about how you told Stephanie not to associate with a certain friend she had known since childhood. Do you believe men have the right to decide who their partners are friends with?

Allen: I didn't decide anything. We've been having this argument for a long time and I think she knows that I'm right. Kate, this friend of hers, is in the bars constantly, and she has a reputation. I think as her husband I have some say in this. After we talked, she agreed with me so it wasn't like I forced her.

Michael: What do the rest of you think? Should Allen have a say in who his partner can be friends with?

Bob: I think both people in a relationship have a right. My wife criticizes my friends all the time.

Toby: Yeah, if his wife's friend is loose it reflects badly on him.

Michael: So when you marry you have the right to give the thumbs-up or thumbs-down to your partner's friends, if you think it reflects badly on you? The marriage contract gives you that authority?

Bob: There has to be compromise and give-and-take in the relationship. And I think if your partner makes a bad decision, you have an obligation to protect her.

Toby: I think it's more an act out of mutual consideration rather than an authority or control thing.

Michael: It seems very controlling to me. I wouldn't like my partner to have that power over my friendship decisions and I don't believe I have the right to interfere in hers.

We spent the entire session discussing this issue with no resolution. Most, but not all, of the men believed it was perfectly acceptable to tell their partners not to associate with certain people. They were either protecting her or protecting their reputations. Most believed that this was a marital responsibility. The next week we took up the theme again, and I asked Allen to participate in a roleplay with me. I would play him and he would play his wife, Stephanie. He reluctantly agreed.

Stephanie (Allen): Allen, I really don't think you're being fair about Kate. Yes, she's divorced, and yes she dates men, but so what?

Allen (Michael): She's a bad influence. I don't trust her.

Stephanie (Allen): It sounds like you don't trust me.

Allen (Michael): I know what it's like when you're with those women. How do I know you won't get tempted being with her, listening to the things that she's saying to you and getting worked up? And I know she thinks I'm an asshole.

Stephanie (Allen): We just have a drink and talk.

Allen (Michael): I told you: I don't trust her and I don't want you to see her anymore! No more discussion!

I ended the role play and asked for feedback from the group.

Bob: Well, if it happened that way, I wouldn't think it would be fair.

Michael: Why?

Bob: She seemed like she was telling the truth.

Others nodded in agreement.

Michael: But earlier you guys said that he had the right to decide what friends she could have if he thought they were a bad influence. Allen, how did it feel being in that position?

Allen: Not good. I didn't mind it so much until you ended it the way you did.

Michael: What did that feel like?

Allen: I felt kinda like a kid.

Accepting your partner's autonomy and independence requires more than just trust. How can you trust your partner if you assume a position in the relationship that gives you the power to decide fundamental issues in her life?

If you have battered and are still in your relationship, remember that healing takes time—and sometimes never happens. Back off. Let her have her own life and allow her the time to sort things out. Trying to isolate her or continuing to isolate her may give you desired results in the short term, but ultimately you will drive her away.

Many of the men I interviewed for this book said that understanding why they had isolated their partners in the past was important for their future relationships. They needed to let go and stop controlling their partners' lives. They had to trust. Perhaps more importantly, they needed to get to a place where they were truly supportive of their partners' aspirations. Today they encourage their partners to have friendships with people. They support their partners' desires to go back to school, change jobs or get a job, take a class, or pursue other activities that make their lives more whole. As their partner's life becomes more satisfying to her, their relationships improve.

From time to time these men probably feel quite threatened. Change can be scary. But as they practice what they have learned, they begin to respond differently. Men who make thorough changes in their relationships know that attempts to control are self-defeating. People *want* to have their own lives. People *need* space to grow independently of each other. Then they can support each other's goals and aspirations, because their union is based on love, concern for each other's happiness, and trust in the relationship.

Using the Children to Get to Her

Unfortunately, many men resort to using their children as weapons against their current or ex-partners. They belittle and undermine their partner in front of the children and to the children. They may threaten to take the children away, or gain custody by saying that their partner is an unfit mother. Sometimes they threaten the children's lives; sometimes they carry out the threats.

Not all men who have battered use their children as a weapon and many men are loving and devoted fathers. Yet all too often, because of the bitterness of the failed relationship or as a tactic to get their way, men make custody threats. Some do it under the guise of love for their children, others base it on their rights as fathers.

For most women, the thought of losing their children is extremely distressing. Men who batter have told me that they have exploited these fears in order to get their partners to drop assault charges or restraining orders. Many women have told me that they stayed in abusive relationships rather than risk losing their children.

As Bernice explains, the threat of losing her children was powerful and made her stay—but the effect on her children was not positive.

"I think my children lost confidence in me because I stayed in an abusive relationship," she said. "I think they felt they couldn't trust me to protect them since I couldn't protect myself.

"The worst thing was that when I threatened to leave him, he said that he would kill one of my kids if I left and I believed him. I stayed longer than I should have because of those threats."

Cassie knows that what her children saw at an early age has long-term implications.

"My kids saw the violence from the very beginning. I was breast-feeding one of my kids and my partner and I got into an argument. He punched me in the nose and blood was flowing all over and my child was screaming.

"I see the impact of the violence on my children all the time. When they get into arguments with each other they get violent. They had to learn that stuff somewhere. My oldest boy never takes responsibility for any of his actions. I know his exposure to his father's constant denial and blame has affected him."

If you have battered, consider the effect your violence has on your children. While you may not be directly abusive to them, their exposure to your violence has a profound effect. Children witnessing domestic assault usually develop some behavioral and health problems, depending on the level of violence they observe. They may have difficulty concentrating in school, become disruptive, or get into fights. Other children from abusive situations have a difficult time trusting people and establishing relationships. Some children blame their mothers for "letting" the violence occur, while others assume responsibility for the violence themselves. They become confused and feel guilty. (11)

As Jim stated at the start of this chapter, the violence he witnessed seemed normal. He tried intervening to stop it, failed, and then learned to adapt. Unfortunately, he then modeled to his children the very behavior he had witnessed.

Children are influenced not only by the violence they observe, but also by the break up of the family. Their stress level increases as they observe the continued hostility between their parents. And they are often put squarely in the middle as their parents struggle, often in court, over custody and visitation.

If your relationship has ended or is ending, try to be as fair and reasonable as possible with your ex-partner. If you are thinking of asking for custody of your children, think also about your motives. Are you seeking custody as revenge on your partner or as a way of maintaining some control over her life? Do you want the responsibility of raising your children? Can

you fulfill it? Would it be in *the children's* best interests to live
with you—or with their mother?

The following discussion about custody occurred with
Grant in one of our groups.

Grant: Angela let me know that she's filing for divorce. I told
her fine, but I'm going for custody.

MaryAnn: Are you going to seek joint custody or full custody?

Grant: Full custody, man.

MaryAnn: You're working full-time, right?

Grant: Yeah, but she's working too. I'll find a way to manage.
I think a man can be just as good a parent as a woman.

MaryAnn: I think men can be wonderful parents. I'm curious,
though, do you know where Angela is going to live?

Grant: Well, her plans are to live with her mother for a while.
I guess her mother will take care of the kids while she's
working.

MaryAnn: I'm asking these questions because I wonder
whether you've been thinking about what would be best for the
children. Your children have been through a lot. I'm just wondering if you've considered what would be the most supportive
environment for the kids.

Grant: Well, in some ways it would be better for them to be
at their grandmother's house. She really loves them and it
would be better than day care. But if Angela gets custody,
pretty soon they won't even know they have a father. She'll
meet some guy and then he'll be in their lives.

MaryAnn: Not having full custody doesn't mean you give up
being their father. You have to decide what kind of father you
want to be, how you want to spend your time with your children
and, ultimately, what is best for the kids.

Even if you have no custodial relationship, you have a thousand and one other things in your relationship with your children which make you a loving and responsible parent. You can take your children to a sporting event, museum, or play. You can provide encouragement and help or join in activities they are involved in: music, scouting, softball, etc. You can take them to special places: a park in the city, or perhaps camping in the country. You can be supportive of your children and help them resolve problems in their lives. Get involved in their school. Show your love, and be the kind of caring father that makes a difference in children's lives.

Whether you or your ex-partner has custody, don't make the children suffer for the problems in your relationship. You may be angry or hurt but you do not have to poison your children. Custody and visitation are often difficult issues, but you and your partner can make decisions that are in the best interests of your children.

In one of our groups, I confronted John about using the children in a manipulative way during visitation.

Michael: John, you said last week that your ex-wife was angry with you because of things you said to the kids when you had visitation. Do you understand why she was angry?

John: I know that last week I was defending my questioning of the children. I know that puts them in the middle. But I still don't want my children exposed to an unhealthy environment. I mean, I think any of the men here would be pissed if their kid's mother was having men overnight. What kind of example is that for the kids?

Michael: It sounds like you're still defending what you did.

John: I know I shouldn't have used the kids that way, but I still believe I have the right to be concerned. I'm not the only guilty one here. The kids tell me the rotten things she says about me.

John's ex-wife Claudia called me about these incidents. She said that the kids were repeatedly asked questions about their mother and that they feel they were interrogated every time John had visitation. She said he implied to them that Claudia was immoral because she had a boyfriend, and that it was her fault that the relationship ended. She also said that her oldest boy was always hostile toward her after spending time with his father.

Obviously, John and Claudia's children are emotionally affected by this behavior. It is true that you cannot keep things from your kids. You cannot hide what is happening in your relationship. However, you should not attempt to use them as allies against their other parent. When John questions his children, they feel guilty if they give too much information and fear what their father will say about their mother. They may try not to take sides or internalize the negative comments that are made, but this is a terribly unfair position in which to put children. Yet this scene gets played out in various ways in far too many divorced families.

Regardless of the anger and resentment you may feel toward your ex-partner, think about the effect your actions and words could have on your children. Be honest with them, but don't abuse their trust. Your children are also victims of the situation. Yet, they are resilient and will heal if you make a commitment to put more care and effort into your relationship with them. Be a good *father.* Keep your issues with your ex-partner separate—and away—from your children.

The Pain of Emotional Abuse

"In order to thoroughly control, you
have to tame the spirit." — *bell hooks*

I am sure you can remember a time from childhood when a parent, teacher, or sibling put you down in some way. If you remember that incident, that probably means you can still feel the hurt. If someone said you were stupid, you may have questioned your abilities. If someone said you were no good, perhaps your self-esteem was diminished. We are all sensitive to the opinions others have of us.

Both men and women can be emotionally abusive. Even in the healthiest relationships, people occasionally reach down into their personal bag of known remembrances, past disagreements, and unresolved issues, and fling a hurtful comment at their partner. Usually when we do this, we are reacting defensively to feeling hurt ourselves. A partner may inadvertently say something hurtful and we respond in kind. However, in a healthy relationship, one partner does not say something that is hurtful or shaming to the other on purpose. Sometimes, confronting one's partner about something can be painful to them, but that is not the same as knowingly degrading or hurting her.

Emotional abuse within the context of battering takes on an entirely different dimension. In the arsenal of battering, emotional abuse is a powerful psychological weapon designed to cause pain, depersonalize the victim, and increase power for the batterer. Men who batter almost always make dehumanizing comments before assaulting their partners. It is easier to rationalize your behavior when you are negatively labeling the people you are hurting. When you call a woman a bitch or a slut you have reduced her standing as a person entitled to consideration and respect.

As Bernice explains, emotional abuse usually accompanies physical violence:

"I hated being called a bitch," she said. "I'd tell him 'I'm not a bitch, a bitch is a female dog.' One time during a bad assault he made me get down on all fours. He said, 'See, you *are* a bitch.' He never totally broke my spirit despite the things he said and did, although, had I stayed with him, he probably would have."

In Cassie's relationship, she started believing the things that her partner was saying:

"I believed the things he told me," Cassie remembered. "He told me that I was ignorant and incompetent. When I first got my job, I thought these people who had hired me must not realize that I'm incompetent. And when he would tell me that no judge would give me custody of the children because I was a bad mother, I believed him.

"When we were intimate, I would tell him personal things. But I always regretted sharing them because he would use them against me. It was almost like he was recording those conversations and waiting for the appropriate time to use them. His name-calling was always hurtful and made me feel less than a person."

Language is one of the prime tools of emotional abuse. What happens when people are called "niggers," "dirty Jews," "savages," or "cunts"? What does it do to our psyche? Not only do we feel direct, incalculable emotional pain, but we also internalize the abuse; the victim begins to believe what is being said.

Paulo Freire wrote: "Self-depreciation is a characteristic of the oppressed, which derives from the internalization of the opinions the oppressors hold of them." (12) In other words, oppressed people feel they are worthless because they accept the hostile opinions of their oppressors as true statements. How does this relate to the impact of emotional abuse on women who are battered? I would like to try and illustrate what I think Freire meant by giving you an example from my life.

I grew up in a community that had its share of anti-Semitism. As a young Jewish boy in a primarily Christian neighborhood, I heard the taunts of other children as they called me "kike," "Christ-killer," and "dirty Jew." These children had not made up these words; they had heard them at home, and in church. Whoever said "Sticks and stones may break my bones but names will never hurt me" was wrong. These derogatory names made me feel that I was a bad person, that I did not belong in "their" neighborhood, and that there was something wrong with being Jewish.

My mother encouraged us to watch films about the Holocaust. These films showed the ghastly details of the extermination camps in Europe. She wanted us to know and be aware of this history. The humiliation, destruction, and confiscation of property, the yellow star, the beatings, cattle cars, gas chambers, and ovens all became images etched in my mind. Why were these people (my people) so despised that something like this could have happened? At my young age, I could not comprehend. During the Christmas season, I felt utterly isolated. Every year our school put on the traditional Christmas programs. The school choirs sang religious songs. In junior high, the entire student body was required to attend the Christmas program. A few students who were Jewish were forced to sit in the principal's office because our parents would not permit us to go. The office was enclosed in glass, and as other students walked by on their way to the auditorium they could all see us, the "outcasts," sitting in the office. Their taunts and embarrassment made me resent being different and, of course, resent my Jewishness.

As I got older, I refused to acknowledge that I was Jewish. If someone made an anti-Semitic remark, I pretended that I had not heard it. I hated being a Jew.

I learned that Jews were hated because of their refusal to accept Christianity. But they were also hated because, throughout history, when there were no quotas restricting Jews from certain occupations, they held powerful positions in the sciences, medicine, education, law, and government. They were often put into roles between the few people in power and the many out of power, as targets for abuse during times of economic or political upheaval. Politically, people on the left and the right assumed we were either international bankers or Communist conspirators or a combination of the two.

My hatred of myself as a Jew began to consume me. I left the United States in 1973 and ironically moved to Germany where I lived for almost a year. I remember driving down the *autobahn* (German freeway) and seeing a sign that read, "Dachau — Next Right." I never stopped at the concentration camp where hundreds of thousands of my people perished in the ovens and gas chambers. Why? Because, as Freire said, I had internalized the opinions that anti-Semites had of me. I did not want to be associated with "those people." This form of self-hatred, based on what I had experienced in my youth, stayed with me for a long time.

I began to change when I came back to the United States. I read books and reflected on this subject and realized other Jews shared similar experiences. When I started working in the domestic violence field, I found some interesting parallels between my denial and lack of self-esteem and women who had been emotionally abused. I hear the stories of women who had been beaten and terrorized, but I also heard many stories in which the put-downs and emotional abuse seemed worse than the physical violence.

As Maria explained in our women's group, emotional abuse can have a lasting effect.

"My partner would have this look on his face and say things like, 'You're nothing but an ugly cunt—no one would ever want you.' If I screwed up, he'd say things like, 'You stupid bitch, you can't do anything right.' At first, I was shocked when he'd say these things. I would cry and usually he would feel bad and apologize. But living with that constant emotional abuse destroyed my self-esteem."

At the domestic violence programs I have been involved with, we attempt to contact the partners of men in our groups. In almost all the interviews we have with these women, I repeatedly hear how their self-image has been damaged, not only by the physical abuse but also by the continued emotional abuse.

Most of the men in our groups admitted that, when angry, they would make the one comment or put-down that they knew would hurt their partner the most. Frank explained that the emotional abuse he used was cruel, but at the time he felt justified.

"I was always into my jealousy stuff with Leila," Frank explained. "Whenever she came home I would really give her the third degree about where she had been and who she was with. If I didn't like the response or didn't believe her, I'd grab her by the hair and say, 'You fuckin' slut, you goddamn whore!' I'd call her sexual names because I knew that hurt her. I was so jealous at that time. I thought, if she hurts me then I'll hurt her back."

Name-calling and put-downs are designed to hurt. They eventually chisel away the spirit and erode self-concept. Much like my experience of self-hatred at being Jewish, many women who are battered begin to believe, or internalize, their abusive partners' opinions of them. Many women indicated that they started believing, or at least doubting themselves about, the terrible things their partners were saying about them. "Why would he say these things if they weren't true?" some of them thought. They began to believe that they were bad mothers or inadequate wives. They questioned their physical appearance. They questioned their abilities and competence.

The combination of name-calling and violence is very powerful. For a man who batters, name-calling and put-downs are often designed to destroy the independence and spirit of the person that he was once attracted to, because those qualities are now threatening. They are threatening because he needs his partner to be dependent on him. If he can make her feel ugly, stupid, or incompetent, she begins to have doubts about herself and her worthiness. With low self-esteem, she may cease to resist the abusive attacks. Resigning herself to the control of an abusive partner becomes her reality.

For some, the kind of disparaging name-calling or put-downs described here do not, or did not, occur in your relationship. Yet, I think it is a rare person who has not said something in anger that he or she wished had not been said.

Throughout this book, I talk about the long healing process that many women must go through after being abused and why, if you are still with the partner you have abused, you need to be patient. I hope that an increased understanding of the impact of emotional abuse will not only increase your empathy, but act as a reminder of how painful words can be. That old saying, "You can't take the words back," is true.

Understanding and Stopping Battering

The Duluth Domestic Abuse Intervention Project created the Power and Control Wheel (on page 81) to illustrate the abusive behaviors used by men who batter to silence, scare, manipulate,

confuse, and control their partners. As stated earlier in this chapter, domestic abuse is more than physical and sexual violence. (If you have difficulty reading the wheel, see the text reproduced in the Appendix.)

The following two exercises are designed to help men understand how they use abusive behavior and how to stop it.

Exercise: The Use of Abusive Behaviors For each behavior on the Power and Control Wheel, review the examples described in each section of the wheel, then think of three to five examples of times that you have used this abusive behavior with your current or former partners. It might be helpful to write your situations down in a notebook or journal.

1. Violence
   a.
   b.
   c.
   d.
   e.

2. Intimidation

   a.
   b.
   c.
   d.
   e.

3. Emotional Abuse
   a.
   b.
   c.
   d.
   e.

4. Isolation
   a.
   b.
   c.
   d.
   e.
5. Using Children
   a.
   b.
   c.
   d.
   e.

6. Minimizing, Denying, and Blaming
   a.
   b.
   c.

        d.

        e.

    7. Using Male Privilege

        a.

        b.

        c.

        d.

        e.

    8. Economic Abuse

        a.

        b.

        c.

        d.

        e.

    9. Coercion and Threats

        a.

        b.

        c.

        d.

        e.

    10. Sexual Abuse

        a.

        b.

        c.

        d.

        e.

Some of your examples may be similar to the ones on the wheel, other behavior may be more subtle. The purpose of generating this list is to illustrate how many different abusive actions are used when you are trying to get your way or stop an argument. Like a basketball player trying new moves and plays to get to the basket, a man who batters and abuses constantly shifts behaviors to control or influence his partner.

Many men in our groups try and minimize their behavior by saying, "I only hit her once." That may be true. But usually these same men fail to recognize the power and impact that their abusive behaviors have on their partners. In our program we tell men that they are still battering unless they stop using *all* the behaviors on the Power and Control Wheel. We say this because, once violence has been introduced to the relationship, everything changes. The other behaviors on the wheel take on an added dimension because your partner never knows when violence may be used again, despite your assurances.

If you are currently in a relationship, I urge you to complete the following exercise inventory to monitor how you may still be using abusive behaviors.

Exercise: Weekly Inventory Try using this inventory every week. Look at the abusive behaviors on the Power and Control Wheel as well as the list you generated. On a weekly basis, take an honest inventory. Think about or write down the behaviors you have used during the past week. Then think about or write down why you used that behavior. Finally, think about or write down how you could have handled the situation differently.

Abusive behavior I used:

_____

_____

_____

What did I want to have happen?

_____

_____

_____

Ways I could have handled the situation differently:

_____

_____

_____

If you are in a relationship now or are contemplating getting involved with someone, pay attention to your reactions to your partner, especially when you are having conflicts. Catch and stop yourself every time you start using abusive behavior to hurt, control, or punish your partner. Seek constructive alternatives. Self-control and making personal decisions about how you will act are your responsibility and yours alone.

4

Getting Past Denial

*Sid's Story — Taking Responsibility —
Minimizing Violence — Self-defense or Retaliation?
— Letting Go of Blame — Alcohol, Drugs,
and Violence — Anger*

In this chapter you will read about how men avoid taking responsibility for their abusive behaviors. You will read how hard it is for some men to see the difference between self-defense and retaliation, and how they minimize their violence. You will also read why some men blame their partners or alcohol for their violence and why all men should dispel the myth that anger is a causal factor in domestic abuse.

In the following story, Sid talks about how he justified his violent behavior. He also talks about the steps he took to change his perceptions of domestic abuse and how he currently lives his life.

Sid's Story

Sid, 42, is a musician and is just completing his law degree. He grew up in Owatonna, a small town in southern Minnesota, and now lives in Minneapolis. He has been public about his past because he wants other men to change. He talked about his battering on the "Phil Donahue Show" and currently conducts groups for abusive men in the Minneapolis/St. Paul area.

I grew up in a middle-class environment in a small town. My father was a plumber and my mother was a homemaker. I was overweight as a youth and consequently my experiences with girls were limited. I had an abusive experience with my first girlfriend. She wanted to break up with me and I was real angry. I called her up and started swearing at her and her dad was listening on the other line. She ended up getting grounded.

Later that month, my buddies and I went to a dance. I heard through the grapevine that my ex-girlfriend was pissed at me because I had gotten her grounded and that she was going to tell me off and slap me at this dance. I remember talking to my friends about how I was going to hit her back, and, of course, they encouraged me not to take any shit from no girl! Well, sure enough she confronted me and slapped me. I punched her so hard that she went flying and her glasses went flying. I felt real exhilarated. My buddies came up and slapped me on the back. I got total reinforcement.

Even though I felt powerful and good, I also felt ambivalent about what I had done. I didn't really want to hurt her, but felt an incredible amount of pressure to protect my honor. I just couldn't let a girl hit me without hitting back.

It was the early 1970s when I married Sharon. We had a child the first year of our marriage. My violence started with me breaking things, smashing chairs, putting my fist through walls, and screaming. I could get her to stop arguing by screaming at her. She would shut up immediately.

This was the "peace and love" time of the sixties and seventies and I didn't feel I had to be accountable to anyone. You know, you do your thing and I'll do mine. Even though we had a child together, I didn't feel very responsible.

I came home one night and Sharon confronted me about not letting her know where I was. I told her I had been out with my friends and she said I was stupid. I told her not to call me stupid and she called me stupid again. She kept calling me stupid and I told her that if she said it again she was going to get it. She was lying on the bed on her stomach and repeated that I was stupid and I punched her in the middle of her back with all my might.

She doubled up and screamed with this incredible pain. I remember her picking up the baby and sitting in a chair, sobbing uncontrollably.

We were married for seven years, and one day she came home with a police officer and took her stuff. We divorced shortly afterward.

I met Rhonda and we started dating. We lived in a small town close to Minneapolis. The violence began right away. She said something that embarrassed me at a party. When we were driving home, I told her that I didn't like what she said. She said I was overreacting and I backhanded her across the face. She was crying all the way home. We got to my apartment and by then she had assumed total responsibility for what happened. She was apologizing and I wasn't budging. I wouldn't accept her apologies, and even though I wasn't angry anymore, I was getting off on her groveling and the pure power of the situation.

The violence would happen every couple of months. On one occasion, I came to her apartment and she was typing something for her college class. I wanted to talk but she told me she needed to finish her work. I started belittling her for going to school and demanded that she talk to me. When she got mad and told me to leave, I became enraged at the rejection. I pushed her over a chair and threw her around the kitchen, slapping and punching her and throwing things. A guy from the downstairs apartment came up to see what was going on and he and I started fighting. I finally left.

The violence got more intense when she wanted to get out of the relationship. One night, we were at a local bar and she talked about breaking up with me. In the middle of the argument, I grabbed her, threw her down on the floor, and started choking her. I didn't stop until people in the bar dragged me off. After that incident, Rhonda slept with a baseball bat under her bed because of her fear of me.

Rhonda and I were in an on-again off-again relationship for 14 years. Despite my violence, the relationship didn't seem unhealthy to me at the time and I'm sure Rhonda didn't think so either. Our relationship and our issues seemed dramatic, but I

certainly didn't see myself as a batterer. Outwardly, I was intellectual. I believed in equality and feminism, and was immersed in
the art culture. In retrospect I can see that I had this outside
posture, but at the time I really felt that women were to be used,
primarily to meet my sexual and emotional needs.

I always thought that the abusive stuff was sort of a glitch in
the relationship. In other words, the relationship would be going
along fine and then we'd have an episode. I felt justified when I
was abusive, because *her* behavior and actions made me angry.
I'd minimize what I did, and when she would confront me I'd say,
"You're crazy."

I'd punch out windows, slam doors, drive fast in the car to
scare her, and pound my fist on the table. The exhilaration of the
outbursts gave me a sense of power. I'd get this rush when I was
abusive. The abuse seemed to underscore my importance. My
behavior seemed like an appropriate response to the situation.

Rhonda was a gregarious person and I was extremely jealous.
I would do what I could to isolate her and keep her from having
contact with other men. I'd do this big guilt and pity thing and say
things like, "You don't give a shit about me."

You really get a lot of support from other men when you're
abusive. I remember one time I put my fist through a window and
had my hand all bandaged up. I went down to the bar and my
friends asked me what happened and I said that I had been
fighting with Rhonda again. No one ever confronted my behavior
as being wrong. Instead they said, "Yeah, those fuckin' women,"
and "Why do you put up with her?"

In the early eighties, I started getting confronted by some of
my women friends about my battering. I had to look at myself,
and what I saw wasn't very pretty. But that confrontation led to a
personal decision and commitment to change. I didn't want to
batter again and I didn't want a woman whom I loved to be afraid
of me.

I hooked up with some other men who wanted to address
men's violence. We met regularly and discussed the origins of our
violence. It wasn't easy to admit some of my behavior to the other
men. The more we met and talked, the more I learned about

myself and the more determined I was to change. I started speaking out publicly about my violence. I think being public is a real motivator for change, whether it's getting confronted by people or getting arrested. There's something very humbling about it.

Even after I committed to not being violent with Rhonda, she was still afraid of me. If I got angry or depressed, I knew she was not sure what might come next. I had to learn to communicate my anger in different ways. I was responsible for her fear because of my past violence, so I felt obliged to alter my interactions with her. If we got into a disagreement, I told her that I wasn't going to be violent. I reassured her and tried to create a safe space.

I'm convinced that my battering was a key reason why my relationship with Rhonda ended. Even though I was committed to being nonviolent, there was a certain level of trust that we could never restore, and we lost a level of emotional spontaneity because of the past.

The *Phil Donahue Show* was doing a program on domestic abuse. I was asked to be on the show because Rhonda and I had told our stories publicly in Minnesota. When I explained that my violence was an attempt to control and punish Rhonda, people in the audience asked, "What did she do to provoke you?" The whole thing about provocation can be seductive. But my violence was a personal choice.

Today, in my current relationship, I have more of an internal dialogue going on. I'm aware of what I'm doing and what I'm saying; it's kind of a self-monitoring process. I listen more. I talk honestly about what's going on in my life. I realize now that when I was abusive I was getting my way but I was also losing out. My partners didn't trust me. They had to be concerned about my moods. They were fearful when I got angry. It's difficult to be intimate when someone is afraid of you.

Men don't understand what kind of fear many women live with—the fear of rape and battering and of being afraid of men. It seems to me that men have to take responsibility and confront our violence.

It has been important to me to disclose to my present partner, Linda, the fact that I battered. I think she has a right to know who she's dealing with. All of this is part of being accountable for my past and my present.

I like working with men and sharing my experiences with them. I guess I think that as men we are kindred in many ways and accept that we each make individual choices. I feel rewarded when men talk straight about these issues and really make some commitments to change. It gives me hope that if men keep talking to men that we can begin to change the attitudes which lead to violence against women. I like being part of the process and this work forces me to continue to examine my own stuff.

Taking Responsibility

Somehow, it just seems like human nature to excuse ourselves when we have screwed up. We do it all the time. If we make a mistake at work, we blame others or the nature of the job. If we respond inappropriately to something at home, we blame our children or our partner. If we are in a bad mood, we blame the world.

It is not easy owning up to our mistakes. We know that "to err is human," yet it is rare to meet someone who has an easy time admitting to being wrong. What a difference it would make if parents, teachers, politicians, professionals, bosses, coworkers, friends, and family members stopped blaming others and took responsibility for their own actions. And that is exactly what men who batter need to do: own up, and take responsibility for their violent behaviors.

Outwardly, society takes a dim view of men beating women. Most boys are taught never to hit girls. Men who are arrested or in some other way publicly confronted with their violence find it difficult to face their friends, family, and society. Many men feel ashamed of their actions, while others feel bad that they were caught. Still others feel self-righteous and justified.

Some men cannot get beyond the excuse that the violence would not have happened if their partner had acted differently. They see their violence as the logical result of a certain situation, and find it difficult to see any alternative. They are full of rationalizations—if she had stopped bitching, not come home late, understood what I was feeling, not put me down, been a better mother, not drunk so much—all blaming statements that provide an excuse for the violence. In one of our groups, Chuck explained an episode that led to his arrest.

Chuck's wife, Nicole, had come home late from an office Christmas party. She had tried calling home, but could not get through. Chuck was supposed to be at his pool league. He could not get a baby-sitter, so he had to wait for Nicole to get home before he could leave, and he was furious.

When she got home, Chuck began insulting Nicole, calling her a goddamn bitch, threatening to beat her up. She responded by telling him to grow up, which further enraged him. He pushed her down the hallway, screaming at her all the way. She attempted to stop his pushing by kicking him. He punched her twice in the head and was subsequently arrested.

MaryAnn asked Chuck to describe his behavior in more detail.

MaryAnn: Chuck, you've just explained the incident to us. You outlined how you felt, how angry you were, and why. Looking back at the way you handled things, can you envision yourself doing things differently in light of everything that has happened?

Chuck: Well, not really. I mean, the kids were home, she had been drinking, and she knew I was supposed to be at the pool league.

MaryAnn: So pushing and punching her resolved that dilemma?

Chuck: I wouldn't have punched her if she hadn't tried to kick me in the nuts. The way I look it at, it was self-defense.

MaryAnn: I'm concerned about how you chose to react to her. Are you saying that you had no other option?

Chuck: Well, I suppose I could have not gone to my league or blown it off. But pool is important to me and she should have been home!

MaryAnn: What about not pushing her down the hallway and not hitting her?

Chuck: I hit her on the side of the head, not in the face, and believe me, it wasn't that hard or she would've been out. The cops had no reason to arrest me.

Chuck had difficulty seeing other options. He could have left the house when Nicole returned and cooled down. He did not have to call her names or push her. And when she tried to kick him, he could have tried to deflect her. He certainly did not need to respond by punching her. Instead of taking any responsibility he blamed Nicole, and downplayed his violence by claiming that he did not hit her that hard.

Often, men seem to have a more difficult time acknowledging personal faults than women, perhaps because of the ways in which they are socialized. Men are brought up to be strong, in control, and "right." Men often think they will be seen as failures if they admit to being wrong or to having problems. As a result, they lie, minimize, or blame others. In Chuck's case, if he was honest, he would have to be accountable to Nicole for what he did. He does not want to be accountable, so he rigidly holds on to the lie that his violence was justified.

Honesty *is* valuable. If you are honest, even if you have done wrong, people judge you far less harshly than you think. You are less alone and people tend to trust you and respond honestly in return. Rather than seeing you as a failure, people respect the fact that you are taking responsibility for your actions and are doing something concrete to make personal changes.

If you are—or have been—violent in a relationship, taking responsibility for your behavior is critical if you are serious about changing. Being accountable is a sincere acknowledgment and acceptance of responsibility. It is not easy, and it is often humbling, but it must be done.

Minimizing Violence

When explaining your violence to others or to your partner, do you sometimes hear yourself saying,

- "It wasn't that bad."

- "I only hit her once."

- "I only slapped her—I would never punch her with a closed fist."

- "She bruises easily."

- "I was drunk."

- "I didn't hit her that hard."

- "This is the first time I've ever done something like this."

- "I just lost it."

These statements may make you feel slightly better, but they minimize the seriousness of your violent and abusive acts against your partner.

Men often downplay an incident to get those who are confronting the violence (police officers, counselors, friends, or a partner) to believe that the abuse was not that bad. The more you downplay what you did, the more difficult it will be to come to terms with your behavior. You will also miss precious opportunities to change.

Morris described the following incident in one of our groups.

"I came home after having a few drinks after work," he said. "I had had a real bad day and I was upset. Paula hadn't made supper and I told her I was hungry. She said she wasn't going to make me dinner because I came home late and because she was watching TV. I started screaming at her. I kicked the TV off the table, grabbed her by the hair, and told her that I should beat the shit out of her. I slapped her and she started screaming because I think she really believed I was going to beat her up.

"I felt that she cared more about that stupid TV show than me. I guess I wanted to let her know that I was hurt. I did feel kind of guilty about slapping her later. The next day I apologized and told her I had been upset about things at work. I also told her that I had been drinking on an empty stomach and that when I felt rejected by her, I just lost it. I mean, I would never really hurt her."

Note how Morris started his explanation by saying he had had a hard day. When he apologized to Paula, he said that he had been drinking on an empty stomach. Then he said he "lost it," when it was quite clear that he was angry because Paula was not doing what he wanted her to do. Morris made a *choice* to become abusive.

Saying "I lost it" or "I lost control" are common ways of describing a violent episode so it appears that it was not really you doing the hitting. The message is that when you get angry something unavoidable happens to you—and you become violent.

But then why don't you lose it at work and hit your boss when he's being a jerk? One reason is you would probably lose your job. If you are upset, depressed, or mad at the world, why don't you lose it on the subway, on the bus, or in a store? Bosses, friends, and strangers are usually not the targets of our violence because there is usually a consequence for that behavior.

Saying that the violence was not that bad also minimizes it, and denies the reality of the person being hurt and abused. Denying or downplaying the incident or blaming your partner for the violence only puts off your accepting full and total responsibility for your use of violence.

Seeing the truth requires not only an honest appraisal of what has happened, but also a willingness to be accountable for your actions. If you want to check whether you have been minimizing your abusive behavior, try a simple test. Ask yourself whether you would want what you did to your partner to happen to you. Would you still say, "It wasn't that bad?"

Self-defense or Retaliation?

A common theme heard in our groups is that the man's use of violence was an act of self-defense. There are many variations of this explanation but in most cases the story is similar to Eric's defense for beating up his wife, Kristen.

> **Michael:** Eric, will you explain your situation again? I'm having trouble hearing you take any responsibility for your actions.
>
> **Eric:** Well, like I said before, I was trying to leave the house. I guess I was trying to teach her a lesson about not bringing in her share of the money. Anyway, she stands in the hallway and tells me I'm not going anywhere.
>
> **Michael:** She's blocking the doorway?
>
> **Eric:** Yeah, more or less. So I get my coat and tell her to get the fuck out of the way.
>
> **Michael:** Did you say anything else to her?
>
> **Eric:** I probably called her a bitch. You know, like, "Get the fuck out of the way, bitch!"
>
> **Michael:** Then what happened?
>
> **Eric:** She slapped me, so I nailed her. I mean I told her, you ever hit me, you're going to get it. You know, it's this double standard, like women can hit men and we're not supposed to hit back. Well, I think that's bullshit. She hits hard. As far as I'm concerned, a man or a woman hits me, I hit 'em back.

Michael: Do the rest of you agree with Eric? If a woman hits you does that give you permission to hit her back?

Many in the group agreed, nodding cautiously, though Tim was not quite convinced.

Tim: Well, I guess it would depend on what you did. I mean, men are a lot stronger and used to fighting than most women I know. I suppose if you slapped her back that would be okay.

Michael: What did you do, Eric?

Eric: I already told you: I nailed her!

Michael: You punched her? Kicked her?

Eric: I punched her.

Tim: How many times?

Eric: This is bullshit. I don't know. A couple of times. And I only hit her once on the side of the head. I mean there were no black eyes or broken bones. She told the cops I kicked her in the stomach and they believed her and now I'm here. Look, I warned her.

Many men feel the way Eric does. He defends his actions by emphasizing that his partner hit him first and then by saying the lack of bruises or broken bones means that he used reasonable force given the situation. He repeatedly uses her slap and his past warnings to justify his violence. In order for Eric to change, he will have to ask himself some hard questions: Was my use of violence really justified? How much physical force do I really need to defend myself? Was this really self-defense? Did I have alternatives?

I use the legal definition of self-defense to describe what is and is not acceptable. According to law, self-defense is the use of force reasonably necessary to prevent imminent injury. Self-defense does *not* authorize a person to seek revenge or punish another. And self-defense does *not* include retaliation. In other words, if your partner throws something at you or slaps you, that does not give you the right to punch her.

Women do use violence in self-defense, and some women initiate violence. At the Domestic Abuse Intervention Project in Duluth, about 10% of the offenders mandated to our program are women, which is consistent with most national research. However, in most cases when a women initiates violence the male retaliates far more severely. Some men have told me that they were glad when their partner hit them, because it gave them permission to beat their partner and feel justified. After all, they think, she hit me first.

As Cassie explains, there is a distinct difference between her violence and her partner's.

> Not that my violence was right, but the impact was totally different. One time, I was furious with my partner. I broke every window in the house with an iron pan—and I mean every window, upstairs and downstairs. I know he must have been scared at the rage that he was seeing because he just stood there. That was wrong and violent.
>
> But on one occasion when we were intimate, I told him that I loved water. I loved rivers and the feel of water on my body. It was my solace. I never thought he would use that against me, but he did. When he was angry with me, he would wait until I got in the shower and then he would come into the bathroom and beat me. One time he hit me so hard, he split my head open. There I was when the police came, naked and bleeding in the bathroom.
>
> After all these years, I am still terrified when I take a shower. I give explicit instructions to the children not to enter the bathroom. I have a clear shower curtain so I can see the door. And to this day, I'm still afraid. When *he* hears glass break, though, do you think he shudders because of that evening when I broke the windows? You can't tell me that my rage and fear are the same as what he experiences.

In my groups, while never condoning violence, I try to differentiate between women's and men's acts of violence and battering. Some of the men in the groups claim that women are just as violent as men. I ask these men to answer the following questions with a Yes or No.

1. Do you ever wait on pins and needles when you hear your partner coming home, wondering what kind of mood she will be in?

2. Does your partner ever strike you for absolutely no reason that you know of?

3. Do you ever fear that you will be asked to have sex with your partner after she has beaten you?

4. Do you flinch when your partner is angry and makes intimidating gestures? Do you fear that her actions are a sign that you will be hit?

5. If you decide to separate from your partner, are you afraid that she will break into the house and beat you? Or try and kill you?

6. Are you afraid of your partner?

Men usually answer no to all of these questions. Some men in our groups even chuckle when I ask them. A woman's use of violence usually differs from a man's because there is an imbalance of power. In addition to a man's physical size, his violence is often accompanied by other battering behavior, which increases his power. He may threaten to kill his partner. He may kill a pet or display weapons in a threatening manner.

Most men who claim they acted in self-defense will later admit that there were alternatives to using violence. These alternatives depend on a person's willingness to remain nonviolent, and are embodied in the following principles that many formerly abusive men have committed to.

1. Violence is not okay unless I am truly in fear of being hurt, and then I should only use as much force as I need to defend myself.

2. In the future, I will be aware of flashpoints—issues or situations where I become agitated or very angry—which in the past have prompted violence by me or my partner.

3. I will leave situations (take a time-out) rather than use violence. (For more about time-outs see Chapter 5.)

4. I will accept the fact that my use of violence is based on my desire to control a situation. I do not always need to be in control, to be proven right, or to win.

5. I will strive toward respectful resolutions of conflicts without being abusive.

Do you believe there are conditions to making these commitments? Exceptions? Do you feel a resistance to accepting them? Committing to these principles is not just an intellectual exercise. These five principles are the foundation for your efforts to remain nonviolent and non-abusive. If you can only agree to them with strings attached, then you have more work to do.

Some women do use violence as a way to punish or hurt their partners. And in some cases men are legitimately fearful of their partners' rage and violence. If you have never used violence or have stopped using it and your partner is engaging in physical abuse, take appropriate steps. Retaliatory violence does not have to be one of them. You can leave, call the police, obtain an order for protection, or seek help from domestic violence programs in your community. Reacting to provocation or violence by echoing it makes it seem as if there are no alternatives.

A note to women: If you are a woman who uses violence against a partner you should be clear about whether you are responding to your partner's violence, defending yourself, or initiating the violence. Talk with friends who will help you to decide which it is. Don't take the blame if the violence is your partner's; say no to it and get away from it. If you find that you are clearly initiating the violence, get help. There are programs or counseling available in most communities, and the resource section at the end of this book lists several organizations that may be helpful.

Letting Go of Blame

It may be difficult to stop blaming your partner for your violence. The following group discussion shows how one group member found it hard to take responsibility for his actions.

Michael: Why do you think it's so hard for us to get beyond blaming our partners for our violence?

Julio: Well, for me, it's just recently that I have seen that I could have acted differently. I mean, I still want to hold on to all the things that Anna did or said.

Michael: So you still believe that she shared responsibility for the violence?

Julio: In my head I know I'm responsible. But when I think about the times I was violent, it's hard to let go of her part in this. I mean, there were times when I thought she was egging me on so I would hit her. Our fights were totally outrageous. I had told her not to push me and she knew I would hit her if she kept going. So when she kept on pushing, I kind of thought that she knew what the consequences were going to be. It doesn't justify what I did, but that's the way I saw it.

Michael: Are you saying that you think Anna wanted to get hit?

Julio: No. But I couldn't understand why she wouldn't just shut up when I warned her to stop. She would say shit that got me so pissed off that I would just lose it.

Michael: So if someone says something that I don't want to hear or says something that hurts or offends me, then it's their fault if I hit them?

Julio: When you say it like that, I would say no. But there are two people in an argument. Are you saying she didn't have any responsibility in this? I mean, I'll own up to my use of violence, but she needs to recognize when she's pushing my buttons.

Michael: I'm not saying that Anna hasn't done or said things that might be inappropriate or hurtful. What I am saying is that regardless of what she says or does, your violence is yours and yours alone. I think it's really important to stop blaming her. You say you've acknowledged your violence, but all your comments have this qualifying statement that says she shares responsibility. Until you come to terms with that, I'm afraid you will remain stuck.

Julio: I hear you. I don't know why I'm having such a hard time letting go of that.

Julio's comment about Anna pushing his buttons makes him sound like a robot whose buttons are being pushed on and off. The whole notion that words can provoke us into using violence is an argument that we must set aside—by our response to the words we make a *choice* to use violence.

Similarly, men who batter frequently believe that their partners should be mind readers, knowing when to approach them and when to leave them alone. Failure to approach them in the "correct" way results in men getting angry and rejecting their partner or hurting her feelings. This can lead to an argument, which may escalate into using violence.

As Cassie states, men who batter often have twisted perceptions of what provokes violence.

"There were times when I would start arguments that resulted in fights," she said. "I mean, we had a lot of issues that caused problems, from money to the children. And I know there were times when I said hurtful or mean things. But when I would bring up a problem we were having, he would say I was provoking him. But I wasn't starting a fight so I could get beat up. Nothing I said gave him the right to do that. He would take any form of communication that made him feel uncomfortable and he would become abusive. Later, he would blame me and say that I had provoked him."

The idea that one's partner provokes the violence is a difficult one to relinquish. Men who batter often believe that their partners are pushing them into conflict. But the conflict usually has more to do with their own anger and resentment over their partner's wanting something or having a different opinion. When their partners assert themselves or disagree, men who batter see their partner's need for autonomy as a hostile provocation.

Andy described his resistance to seeing the truth and accepting responsibility for his behavior.

"I'd hang on real rigidly to my position and try to convince other people that my partner brought the violence on," he said. "I'd say, 'I'm not to blame here. Yeah, I did some stuff, but it's a two-way street. There are two people in this relationship.' I hung on to that. I hung on to that for dear life. I finally started to change when I let go of that and realized that she didn't have to change for me to change. And she wasn't to blame for my behavior, and I alone was responsible for my violence."

Alcohol, Drugs, and Violence

Being under the influence of alcohol or drugs is a common explanation for violent behavior from men who have assaulted their partners. Fifty percent of men who enter the Domestic Abuse Intervention Project in Duluth were drinking or using drugs when they used violence against their partners. While research indicates that men under the influence are likely to batter more severely, it is dangerous and wrong to use alcohol or drug abuse as an excuse for violence.

Russ, a former police officer from Chicago, met with me to enroll in one of our groups. He was upset as he told his story.

Russ: Last night I punched my wife, Lynn, and began to

choke her. I was totally drunk and just lost it. I've never done anything like that before.

Michael: Is she okay?

Russ: Yes. I mean, I think so. She's at the women's shelter. I've been trying to get in touch with her.

Michael: Tell me more about what happened.

Russ: Well, I was really drunk and I just flipped out when she got home. I don't remember everything, but I was on top of her and I was choking her. And then she lost consciousness and I let go. When she came to, I tried to apologize. I mean I would never, never do something like that if I was sober. I'm not that kind of a person. I must have been in a blackout or something, because I was totally out of control. Anyway, she was crying and upset and wanted to go but I wouldn't let her. I must have passed out, because when I woke up, she was gone.

Michael: You say you were totally out of control. Why do you think that you didn't kill her? I mean, you stopped choking her. As drunk as you say you were, as out of control as you say you were, you stopped choking her.

Russ: I don't know. Something snapped, I guess. I'm very confused.

For Russ, alcohol functions as an excuse. The use of alcohol is a way for him to cope with, and try to explain away, his violence. There are two problems, however, with using drug or alcohol abuse as an excuse for violence. First, there are men who deliberately drink to excess to give themselves permission to become abusive. Many times the purpose is to bring up certain situations or issues that are hurtful or unresolved. Getting drunk or high with the intent of entering into a confrontation with a partner is a set-up for abuse. After the violence, the man can chalk the situation up to being drunk or stoned, and say to himself, "It wouldn't have happened if I'd been sober."

The second problem with accepting alcohol and drug

abuse as an excuse for violence is that society, friends, and family—and often the mental health community—may view alcohol or drugs as the primary problem. Many people assume that if they resolve a substance abuse problem, they will end their abusive and violent behavior. This is a dangerous idea for the partner of an abusive man. People who abuse alcohol or drugs and act violently have two problems—not just one. They need to address *both*.

Unfortunately, substance abuse treatment usually does not address the reasons for a person's violence. In many cases, men will continue to batter when they are sober.

If you think you have a substance abuse problem, take immediate short-term steps, whatever is necessary, to ensure you will not be in a position to act out violently. Then get an assessment on substance abuse and follow the recommendations of your counselor. This may mean going into in-patient or out-patient treatment, followed by aftercare. After completing that treatment you can begin a program that deals specifically with the issues of violence. The two programs have two very different functions, even though some of the issues you deal with will overlap.

A note to women: If your partner is both violent and under the influence of alcohol or drugs you are at risk to suffer serious injuries. Call a shelter in your area immediately or use the resource section at the end of this book to find other places to get help.

Anger

Anger is a common human emotion. We get angry at people, events, and ourselves. If someone cuts in front of us on the freeway, if our children do something wrong, if things at work are difficult, or if events in the world are troubling, we may get angry. This is a normal feeling and not necessarily a negative emotion.

However, men who batter often cite anger at their partner

as the reason for their violence. This discussion in one of our men's groups shows how Calvin uses anger to justify his violence.

Calvin: I decided to come to this group to get a handle on my anger problem.

Michael: What do you mean by "anger problem?"

Calvin: Well, when I'm in a relationship with a woman and she does something that pisses me off, sometimes I get violent. I want that to stop.

Michael: Are you saying that anger causes the violence?

Calvin: If I wasn't angry I guess I wouldn't be violent.

Michael: Does that mean that if you get angry with me right now you're going to hit me?

Calvin: No. You don't understand.

Michael: What don't I understand?

Calvin: There are certain things that get people angry, and then that triggers a violent response. My past girlfriend would say things that got me so angry that I became violent. I suppose if you said certain things I could get that angry with you.

Michael: It seems to me that you're making a choice when, and with whom, you're going to be violent when you get angry.

While anger does not cause violence, it is an emotion many men use when things are not going their way. People get angry with each other in most relationships, but men who batter typically use anger as a way to control their partners and show displeasure. Most women resist being controlled, yet men who batter try to impose their ideas of what should happen regardless of their partner's resistance. They perceive their partner's refusal to abide by the rules they have designed for their partner and the relationship as defiance or provocation, and get angry. Their expressions of anger are followed by threats, intimidation, and violence. Then they blame the violence on their anger.

Women who live with abusive men quickly learn to watch for mood swings and either accommodate their partner's rules or resist them.

We often believe we need to express our disapproval through angry words or actions. If this becomes a common pattern we develop a tendency to lash out. Lashing out in turn can bring an initial and often exhilarating rush. Screaming, punching a wall, calling someone a name, or hitting someone lets off steam and gets attention. However, venting anger in such an intimidating way is threatening and unfair to others.

Some people feel bad or foolish after going into a rage and may try to make amends for their behavior. They walk around feeling guilty and powerless to confront this seemingly sudden and uncontrollable rage. Others find a sense of power in unleashing and venting their anger and feel no remorse. They walk around angry at the world, expecting someone to cross them. Then they can vent without taking responsibility.

I am not suggesting that you should never get angry. But do find an appropriate way to express anger. As with other emotions, you can feel and express anger in a healthy, nonhurtful manner. But you must have a clear understanding of the patterns that occur when you get angry before you can change them. If your usual response after getting angry is to explode at someone, remove yourself from the situation before you say or do something abusive.

It is important that you not confuse the emotion of anger with your choice of becoming abusive. Explaining your violence by saying, "She made me so angry I . . . " is a convenient—but dishonest—excuse.

As you address the ways you deny or minimize your abusive behavior and as you stop blaming others for your violence, you will begin to see more clearly what you really *do* when you become violent. Then you can begin to move ahead and make real changes in your life. In Chapters 5 and 6, you will read about concrete ideas and suggestions to help you to change and heal.

5

Making Changes
and Staying on Track

Mark's Story — Letting Go — Taking Time-outs —
Self-talk: Learning to Think Positively — Handling
Jealousy — The Danger of Obsession

In this chapter, you will read about letting go of relationships that have ended, some important exercises to help you stay non-abusive, including time-outs and positive self-talk, and handling jealousy and obsession.

Mark's Story

Mark, 28, is an environmental engineer and lives in an upper middle-class suburb of St. Paul. He is presently separated from Jody, the woman he battered. Their divorce is pending. In his story, Mark talks about his abuse and the struggle it has been to put his life back together. At the time of the interview he was attending a domestic violence group in the Minneapolis/St. Paul area.

> My parents never fought. Throughout my childhood, I only re-member one incident where they had a verbal confrontation. We lived in a nice neighborhood and had a beautiful home. My par-ents rarely hit us. I think I was spanked on one occasion.

I'm not sure what influenced my violent tendency. I guess it had something to do with my size; I'm not very big. I would get picked on in school a lot and I started to fight back. I started to get into a lot of fights and I think that shaped my attitude about violence.

I felt powerful when I got into fights. It also got me acceptance from the guys I wanted to hang around with. At the time I liked that tough-guy image. I thought that it might impress the girls, but in retrospect I think they thought we were being childish.

Jody and I got married right after high school and we were together for about ten years. The first couple of years of our relationship were pretty good. I joined the Marine Corps and Jody and I moved to California. After I got out of the service, we moved back to the Twin Cities.

Looking back, I don't think I really wanted to be married. I was young, and all of a sudden, I was married and had a kid on the way. I resented the responsibilities of marriage. I got this job that required a lot of traveling, and that caused conflict. I liked being on the road because I didn't want to be that involved with Jody and I liked the freedom.

One time, Jody called me at a hotel and told me I had to come home right away. When I got home, she told me that she wanted me to find a job close to home and that she couldn't stand my traveling anymore. A couple of weeks later the bombshell hit: she told me that she had had an affair. It hit me like a ton of bricks. She said she only slept with the man once and the relationship was over, but the incident changed everything.

After the affair, I started treating Jody differently. What I said went. I'm sure some or most of my behavior was punishment. Even though I tried to put it behind me, I couldn't. I started making all the decisions in the relationship, from what movie we saw to what groceries we would buy.

To get back at her, I started lying to her to make her suspicious. Sometimes I wouldn't come home at night to piss her off. When she went out, I would interrogate her when she got home. She had to account for her entire evening, including who she was with and where she went. Sometimes I would check the mileage on the car to see if she was telling the truth.

The first time I was arrested for assault was about three years ago. We were driving home and she wanted to stop and get something to eat, but I refused to stop. We argued all the way home. She kept saying how I always got my way and how I always made the final decision. We got home and she said something derogatory to me. I grabbed her and pushed her into the wall. I was clearly in a rage and she was totally shocked.

She went into the house and called the police. I followed her and hung up the phone but she had gotten through to them. I took the wedding pictures off the wall, smashed them on the floor, and started swearing at her. I broke other things in the house. She went to the other room hoping that I would calm down. I grabbed a couple of knives from the kitchen and threw them at the wall, partly out of just being pissed and partly to scare her.

When the cops came I started to fight with them. I had one of the cops pinned on the floor; another cop maced me. By that time, there were several officers at my house and they arrested me.

My daughter saw the entire incident and I know it had a big effect on her, especially when the police arrested me. For some time after that, whenever she saw a police car she would say things like, "Remember when the police came to our house and took you away? I don't like police." I didn't talk to her about the incident and would change the subject when she brought it up.

I spent the night in jail and my lawyer picked me up in the morning. When I got home from jail, I could tell that Jody was nervous. I apologized for what I had done and we talked for a while. I told her I would go to counseling, but I never did. I didn't want to go to a domestic-abuse program because of the stigma of saying you've beaten your wife. With my circle of friends, it would be better to have been arrested for bank robbery than for domestic assault.

Both my lawyer and I asked Jody to write a letter to the court stating that the incident was exaggerated, and she did. By the time the case went before the judge our relationship was going pretty good. I was on my best behavior during that time because I didn't want to go to jail. I think the fact that Jody wrote that letter and that both of us stated that we wanted to make the relationship work influenced the judge. The assault charges were dropped. I never thought that the violence was that bad. My friends, family, and my lawyer supported me. I would bring up the affair she had had and they would side with me. I guess they felt I was justified in what I was doing and that some men would have done a lot worse. My lawyer would say there's nothing wrong with throwing things around in your own house. With everyone defending me, I felt like the victim of this bitch and of the police who were overstepping their authority.

I was never intoxicated when I abused Jody. In fact, I rarely drank very much.

Jody and I went to a marriage counselor a couple of years later. The issue of my violence rarely came up. When the counselor asked specific questions about the violence, both Jody and I would minimize the abuse.

I would smash things in the house when I was angry or when I wanted to scare her. If I became upset at something she'd said, I would step on her foot and put all my weight on her. She would always cry when I did this because it hurt, but I felt justified because I thought she was hurting me by yapping and embarrassing me in public. Sometimes I would pinch her really hard, usually under the table if we were out with people, to get her to shut up. I would tell her that I was going to kick her ass and sometimes I would threaten to kill her.

I think the emotional abuse was the worst part of it. Jody was very sensitive about her weight even though she really wasn't that big. I'd call her "fat ass." Sometimes I'd get in her face and say, "You fuckin' bitch, I'm so sick of you!" I'd tell her that I hated her and she would go into the bedroom and cry. I would say anything that I could think of to hurt her.

I hated the way things were going in my life. I knew what I was doing was wrong, but at the time I couldn't see alternatives. I got into this pattern of being real abusive to her. I mean, it got to a point where I felt almost funny when I was nice to her.

I don't know why we stayed together so long. I guess we both hoped things would change. The last incident occurred about a year ago. Jody had decided to leave. She wanted me out of the house while she was moving out. I came to the house after work. I wanted to talk to her about whether we were actually going to split up. She didn't want to talk and asked me to leave. She was sitting on the floor folding laundry with her back to me. I came up behind her and grabbed her by the hair. I pulled her up off the ground and started shaking her. I demanded that she talk to me.

She was scared because I caught her by surprise. I screamed in her face, "I ought to kill you, you goddamned fuckin' bitch." I pushed her down on the floor and left. She called the police and I was informed the next day that I was charged with assault. The charge was subsequently dismissed after I hired my slick lawyer again to get me off.

Even though our relationship is over, I've still been abusive. Jody is seeing a man and I've questioned the kids about what she is doing, which I shouldn't do. It makes me feel bad that she's already seeing someone else.

My trust with women is pretty low. But I know I need to get on with my life, and I'd like to get involved in a new relationship. I may need to continue in counseling for a while and I'm certainly not going to rush into a relationship until I'm ready. I guess I've really seen the light since being in the program. I don't want anyone else to experience the pain that Jody experienced from me and I don't want the pain myself. Relationships don't have to be like this.

I'm not sure that I want to tell a new partner about my past violence. I don't believe I'll ever be violent with a woman again. If things aren't working, I'm confident I'll leave or get help before things ever get to that point. Perhaps there will come a time when I can talk freely about it, but it's too fresh right now.

I feel better today and I'm starting to get my life together. Despite the affair, I really believe that I caused the marriage to break up. I'll always be mad about that. I'm trying not to get into a pity thing about where I'm at—you know, the poor-me syndrome. Living alone has not been easy. I'm often lonely, but I'm dealing with it. I know this is going to sound weird, but I wish I would have been sent to the Domestic Violence Program after my first arrest five years ago. I'm convinced my relationship would be alive today because my whole attitude would have changed. It's too bad I had that slick lawyer.

Letting Go

Mark is nearing the end of his domestic abuse groups. Unlike the other men who have told their stories, he is still sorting through the past and the hurt. His abusive behavior was relentless and clearly punitive after Jody's affair. For five years he made her pay—and they both suffered.

People often have painful experiences in relationships. Communication breaks down, conflicts surface over children, money, sex, and commitment, and affairs happen.

Sometimes people seek affection and love elsewhere because a relationship is emotionally bankrupt and intimacy is gone. For others, an affair is a one-time thing; afterward, guilt sets in and the affair is seen as a mistake.

An affair in a monogamous relationship can be crippling, as it was with Mark and Jody. Some relationships survive, however, and people rebuild their trust and continue to work on their relationship.

Many men in our groups tell me that, in retrospect, they should have ended their relationships much sooner. The love and intimacy was long gone, but they stayed because of the children, or for fear of being alone, or for financial reasons. Violence adds a confusing component to all this; sometimes it prolongs a dying relationship, and sometimes it hastens its demise.

I do not believe a couple should consider divorce every time their relationship hits some ruts in the road, but I also do not believe in hanging on when it is time to let go. Frequently, at the end of a relationships, one or both parties are ambivalent. Seeing a counselor and being truly honest about your feelings may help clarify whether you want to make the relationship work or not.

If you have battered your partner, however, couples counseling may not be appropriate unless the violence has stopped and your partner feels safe to talk freely without fear of retribution. You should not pressure or coerce your partner to attend counseling. She may need time and support from outside sources, like battered women's advocates and support/education groups for women, before she is ready to attend marriage counseling with you. Honor her requests.

Letting go of a relationship is always hard. Confusion over what went wrong and conjectures about how you might have handled things differently can be consuming and debilitating. Do not pretend that the feelings do not exist. Feel them and understand that this is a natural process. The feelings will slowly pass and you will get on with your life.

Try, through the process of self-talk discussed later in this chapter, to dislodge any bitter feelings and thoughts about your partner. Those feelings and thoughts are not helpful and get in the way of healing and letting go. Similarly, do not wallow in guilt and shame about the past. Think through the past in phases and do not expect clarity right away. The grieving process may obscure a clear picture of all that worked and all that did not in the relationship.

In subsequent sections of this chapter on self-talk and jealousy, we will explore the letting go process in more detail. However, if you feel desperate about losing a relationship, seek help from a counselor. Develop a plan to stop focusing on your former partner. Part of the plan may include finding new activities so you do not feel isolated. Counseling and support groups will help you to let go and move on with your life.

Taking Time-outs

Taking a time-out means removing yourself from an explosive situation. This practice may seem simplistic and it is—but it works.

You take a time-out any time you feel you may become abusive. You make a commitment to remove yourself from a situation that might otherwise result in your intimidating, threatening, emotionally abusing, or hitting your partner.

When people get angry, it is usually because they are not getting what they want or because someone is doing something they do not like. Taking a time-out does not address the *causes* of your anger, but it does provide an instant tool to help you avoid situations where you might become abusive.

When you get angry or agitated, you usually have emotional or physical feelings. On an emotional level, you may feel hurt, defensive, or mad. Your mind becomes engulfed with anger and you feel an urge to vent your feelings. On a physical level, you may feel your fists or teeth clenching together, a tightness in your stomach or neck, tenseness in the body, or headaches.

These emotional and physical feelings are cues that anger and possibly violence are on the way. Pay attention to these cues. When you feel that you cannot express yourself in a non-abusive manner, take a time-out and leave.

You can use a time-out to get away from a potentially abusive situation, such as an argument between you and your partner that is about to begin or that has escalated. Perhaps you have been thinking about present problems or past issues and feel yourself getting angry. Recognize the emotional and physical changes in yourself, listen to what your body is telling you, and get ready to take a time-out.

What to Do and Where to Go During Time-outs

First, calmly tell your partner (or write a note) that you are taking a time-out. You might say, "I'm feeling angry and I need to take a time-out." By stating this clearly you let your partner know that you are taking responsibility for your actions and leaving to avoid anger that may result in abusive behavior.

Second, let your partner know how long the time-out will last. You might say, "I'm feeling angry and I need a time-out. I'll be back in one hour." Never stay away longer than you have indicated without calling to let your partner know. This is so that your partner is not scared or startled when you return and also is not left wondering when you might return.

During your time-out, do not use alcohol or drugs. Do not drive. Take a walk; that is usually the best way to relax. You may also want to talk with a friend or someone from a support group, if you are in one. Whatever the conflict, use the time-out to think positively about yourself, your partner, and the relationship. Remind yourself that you are a good person, that your partner is a good person, and that separately or together the two of you will be able to resolve the conflict in due time.

Many conflicts between partners arise over little issues that are blown out of proportion, generally because of the mood one of the partners is in. When you take a time-out for what may be a minor misunderstanding, try to separate your emotion from the issue and tell yourself that your anger, too, will pass.

Sometimes, though, conflicts arise between partners because of major differences or large, unsolved issues. These might include money problems, jealousy, sex, the children, or disagreements about decisions that affect both of you. Obviously, these issues need time, discussion, and negotiation. You should still take a time-out if, during discussion and disagreement, you believe you may become abusive. In this situation, a walk and positive self-talk may be useful in the short term. In the long term, however, you may need to do other things to work out the problem, including setting up an environment where negotiation can proceed fairly, without intimidation and threats and in a true spirit of give-and-take. You may also consider seeing a counselor to help you iron out the problem.

Regardless of the difficulty of the issue, take a time-out every time you recognize your cues. Let your partner know what you are doing, and leave before you raise your voice or do anything that may make your partner afraid.

Although I recommend taking time-outs to the men in my groups, I am also aware that some men use them to avoid working on problems. If you take a time-out every time you have a disagreement, your actions would not only be controlling but self-defeating. Use time-outs with a constructive purpose in mind.

Time-out Rules

1. Take a time-out when you recognize your cues and before your anger level escalates.

2. Take a time-out when you feel like you want to become abusive; do not take a time-out to avoid conflict.

3. Tell your partner you are taking a time-out.

4. Tell your partner how long you will be gone.

5. Do not drink, use drugs, or drive.

6. Call a friend or group member for support.

7. Do calming exercises like walking, shooting free throws at a basketball court, or meditating.

8. Think positive thoughts. Do not dwell on the problem that caused you to become angry.

9. If you are still agitated and need more time than you agreed to, call your partner and let her know.

10. Your partner is not obliged to take a time-out; you take a time-out for *yourself.*

11. If your partner indicates that she is afraid of you, stay away. Find an alternative place to stay until things have calmed down.

12. When you return, do not insist that you and your partner should solve or resolve the conflict you were having.

13. If you notice your cues again, take another time-out.

14. Whenever you follow the time-out rules, make a note of the positive way you handled the situation and its results.

An important note: If you are going to use time-outs in your relationship, review this section and the previous one with your partner. You may want to practice a time-out when you are not angry so that you and your partner understand the process and each other's expectations. Your partner needs to know the rules of the time-out so she knows what to expect.

Self-talk: Learning to Think Positively

Self-talk is that internal voice with which you talk to yourself. It is part of an internal thinking process, and in some ways is like a little tape recorder in the mind that continually plays positive or negative messages.

If you feel anxious, jealous, insecure, or angry, you are usually thinking negatively about a situation or person. Maybe things in your life seem hopeless. Then the tape plays negative messages like: "I'll never get that job—I just don't have the skills"; "She doesn't really care about me, I'm wasting my time"; "I'm no good—everything I do comes out bad"; or "I'll never be happy, I might as well stop trying." If you continue to focus on these negative thoughts and don't resolve the problem, you can become seriously depressed. And you may start taking out your negative feelings on others, especially family members.

The use of positive self-talk is a process of replacing negative messages by concentrating on positive thoughts like, "I am a good person"; "I know I'll succeed if I keep trying"; "I have no reason to be jealous"; and "This problem (like other problems) will pass." You may need to repeat these statements many times to erase the negative thoughts. Positive self-talk, like most changes, takes time, will, and concentration.

The following is an example from our group of how positive self-talk can work. Steve's usual response to conflict was to storm around, swear, and yell. I asked him to practice positive self-talk the next time a conflict occurred and to express his anger in an appropriate manner. He agreed.

In one of the following group sessions, Steve told us about how he used self-talk to avoid becoming abusive. He said he was angry because his partner got home late with the car, which meant that he was late for his golf game. In the past, Steve said that he would have been "all over her" as soon as she walked in the door.

"I was really mad as I waited for her," he continued. "I made a couple of calls, but I couldn't locate her. I was getting madder and madder, but I tried the positive self-talk approach. Every time a negative thought came into my head like, 'She doesn't give a shit about me,' I replaced it with a thought like, 'There must be a good reason why she's late.'

"I then called my golfing partners and told them that I would be late and would catch up with them. When Patricia got home 45 minutes late, I sat at the table rather than rushing to the door. She was nervous when she came in because of my past behavior, but I didn't look angry (at least that's what she said). I calmly asked her where she had been. Normally, I would have been screaming things like, 'Don't you know I've got plans?' But I waited for her response, which was apologetic and reasonable. Seeing that she wasn't afraid of me felt good. I guess I don't have to be an asshole every time I get mad."

Another example of changing negative tapes and practicing positive self-talk came up in our group. Jerry had been making it hard for his partner, Joan, to go back to work. MaryAnn questioned him about this.

MaryAnn: Jerry, you were talking last week about how you didn't want Joan to go back to work. What's been happening?

Jerry: We've been talking. I told her that I would try and be supportive, but she knows that I don't want her to go.

MaryAnn: Did you tell her that you didn't want her to go?

Jerry: I guess I've been pretty indirect and manipulative. I tell her that I'm okay with her decision, but then I tell her that I make enough money for both of us. I'm sure I come off as suspicious.

MaryAnn: Why are you so resistant to her getting a job?

Jerry: Well, she used to work at this restaurant years ago and there were lots of men there. I remember when we were dating, she would go out with her coworkers after work and have drinks and a good time. I don't know, I guess I'm assuming I'll be jealous, and we've had some rocky times, you know.

MaryAnn: My hope is that you would accept her decision and support Joan. We've been talking about self-talk the last couple of weeks. Maybe the group could come up with some ideas on how Jerry could change the negative messages he has when he thinks about Joan going back to work.

The group came up with the following ideas for self-talk which Jerry could substitute for his negative and suspicious thoughts.

- Joan needs to have her own life.

- She will be happy.

- If I don't control her she will respect me more.

- I have my work life, she should have hers.

- I don't need to be jealous.

- The extra money will be helpful.

- I need to remember what I've learned in the group.

- I should trust her.

MaryAnn: Jerry, when the negative thoughts occur, try to use some of these statements. If you need to, repeat them in your mind and believe them.

Jerry: I'll give it a try.

Exercise On Self-talk Practice self-talk yourself. Think of an issue in your life that evokes negative feelings. What are your concerns? If it helps, write down your negative thoughts. Now think of examples of positive self-talk to counter the negative ones. Write down these positive messages. When the negative thoughts creep into your mind, use your positive self-talk messages to push the negative ones out.

It helps greatly to use positive self-talk when you take a time-out, because during this time you are usually worked up. The best approach to a time-out is to take a long walk, take long deep breaths, and repeat the self-talk statements from your list.

We cannot "will" our problems to go away, but we do not need to dwell on them and have them consume us. There are things in life over which we have no control, but we *can* control our reactions to them.

Handling Jealousy

Men and women get jealous. In fact, jealousy is a very common emotion that most of us have experienced, probably quite often. Yet, for some men, jealousy becomes a life-consuming passion that distorts reality. Jealous people question everything their partners do and feel: their trust, fidelity, love, and commitment. They get jealous if their partner buys new clothes, puts on make-up, or gets a new hairstyle. They get jealous if she talks on the phone, writes letters, or goes out with friends. In our groups these men constantly blame their partner's unfaithfulness for their violence—even though their suspicions are often unjustified.

Feelings of jealousy are tied to the belief that one partner has a right to control the other, and to possessiveness, which brings problems into any relationship. Many men enter a relationship feeling extremely possessive, and become jealous and suspicious right away if their partner's behavior does not conform to their expectations. This does not even give the couple time to discuss what they expect from each other in the relationship.

Jeff told the following story in one of our groups.

Jeff: Arlette and I had been arguing pretty much all night about her going bowling with this group of friends. I didn't used to mind, but there are these women in this group that I just don't trust.

Michael: Why?

Jeff: Everyone knows that they are pretty loose. One of them is single and the other recently divorced, so . . . .

Michael: So what happened?

Jeff: Well, like I said, we were arguing about her going and I was pretty insistent that she not go. I mean part of it was her friends, but we had also been drinking and I didn't want her to drive. When she tried to leave, I blocked the doorway. Then she tried to go out the back door and I grabbed her by the arm and slapped her and took the keys out of her hand.

Michael: Was the real issue the fact that she had some drinks or that you didn't want her to go bowling with her friends?

Jeff: Both. But I guess I was mostly reacting to her being with those women. Anyway, she was pretty upset. But I think on some level she knew I was right. We talked about it later that night.

Michael: What kind of feelings were you having about her going?

Jeff: I suppose I was feeling somewhat insecure and scared, and had she gone I would have been worried.

Michael: Of what?

Jeff: That being with those women would give her ideas. That maybe she would find some other man there and sleep with him. I don't really know, except I felt insecure.

Michael: So you hit her and stopped her from going. I'm curious. Did those feelings of being scared and insecure go away by forcing her to stay home?

Jeff: That night I didn't have those feelings. But later I had them again because I knew that I was depriving her of doing something that she really enjoyed. So I've been thinking that Arlette must really think I'm a jerk or something, and then those nervous feelings come back.

In this case, Jeff used violence to control his partner and end a disagreement. He succeeded in one respect, because Arlette did not go out. But looking at the long-term impact of his actions, we see that the very feelings that he wanted to avoid— fear and insecurity—were intensified. He told the group that he became even more jealous later. He finally accepted Arlette's going out with her friends, in part because he knew she was angry at him for trying to stop her, yet he always made an issue out of it the night she was to go out. Jeff also admitted checking up on her, because his insecurity and jealousy were so intense.

As much as Jeff tried to justify what he was doing, he was aware of his partner's unhappiness, and his mind kept conjuring up the worst. Every time he made an arbitrary decision about her life he imagined her thinking about leaving him for someone who would treat her better. As his insecurity grew he became more controlling. He used a variety of threats, including the possibility of taking his own life. The abuse became an endless cycle until finally his partner left him.

Handling jealousy is not easy, but it is possible. If you continually have jealous feelings, talk to friends, practice self-talk, or see a counselor. The best way to keep from being destructive is to put the situation into perspective. Your partner's right to have friends and spend time as she wishes does not have to make you feel jealous. And if someone finds your partner attractive, it does not have to be threatening.

Trust is earned and develops over time; it cannot be imposed by making demands or controlling another person.

The Danger of Obsession

For some men, the thought of losing a relationship is unbearable, and their jealousy becomes an obsession. They think about their partners all the time. They may try to think about something else, yet images of their partner with another person slip into their minds, setting off feelings of anger and pain. They cannot imagine living without this person.

An obsession can be destructive and is often dangerous. We frequently read newspaper articles about an estranged husband killing his ex-wife, family members, and then himself. There is a difference between feeling jealous and having an obsession about someone. If you are jealous, you may be concerned or even afraid that your partner is interested in others or that others are interested in your partner. Jealousy can usually be resolved through honest communication, reassurance, and trust. An obsession, on the other hand, is an intense preoccupation with losing a partner. These compulsive feelings and emotions are usually unwanted, but frequently consume the person who is obsessing.

While a jealous person still has contact with reality, an obsessive person has lost or can easily lose touch with reality; he is operating in a fantasy world in which anything is excusable to avoid losing the object of his obsession.

If you find yourself enmeshed in obsessing about a relationship that has ended or may end, if you cannot stop thinking about your partner, or if you feel you cannot live without her, get help at a mental health agency in your community. A counselor can help you sort through your feelings, gain some perspective, and move on in your life. Sometimes, when a relationship ends you think that you will never get through the pain. Your feelings are feelings of loss and you need to grieve just as you would if someone close to you died. A counselor can help you cope and get through this period, too.

A note to women: Men who are obsessive about holding on to a relationship can be dangerous. If your partner or ex-partner makes threats like, "If I can't have you, nobody will," get help *immediately.* If your ex-partner follows you, threatens your friends, checks up on you, sends unwanted letters, or calls your home against your wishes, you could be in danger. Seek assistance from a battered women's shelter, obtain a protection or restraining order, or develop a safety plan, which may include going to a safe home or moving to a different area. Call the police and let them know what is occurring. *Never* disregard indications of obsession, especially if there has been violence in your relationship.

A note to counselors: If you are providing counseling to a man who is obsessing about the loss of a partner, or to a woman who has concerns about a partner's obsession, probe to assess the possibility of lethality. Find out:

1. Is he depressed?

2. Has he threatened suicide?

3. If yes, does he have a plan? Does he possess weapons?

4. Has he threatened to kill her?

5. Is he preoccupied with her or does he follow her around?

6. Is he on medications or has he ever been hospitalized?

7. Is he isolated or cut off from friends and family?

8. Does he believe that he owns her?

9. Does he idolize her?

10. Does he abuse alcohol or drugs?

While all of these warning signs should be taken seriously, usually a cluster of these behaviors increase the danger that an individual may commit a homicide. We cannot predict who will kill, but we *can* be attuned to signs.

If you are providing counseling to a man who has an obsession, you may want to seek further evaluations. He may need to be hospitalized. Get information about your options, which may include notifying authorities. Call the victim and let her know your concerns. Encourage her to call a battered women's program and develop a safety plan. Remember, you have a duty to warn. If you believe that your client is a threat to another person, you must take the appropriate steps to protect that person.

Similarly, if you are working with a woman who expresses concern about her partner's or ex-partner's obsession, make sure you refer her to a local battered women's program and assist her with safety options. Your attention and action is critical and may save her life.

6

Resolving Conflicts, Strengthening Relationships

Elliot's Story — New Relationships, Old Problems —
Egalitarian Relationships — Sharing the Load —
The Issue of Money — Expressing Feelings —
Learning to Negotiate and Compromise

People have conflicts even in the most stable relationships. How we choose to resolve our differences is frequently influenced by the behaviors modeled for us when we were growing up. For men who are violent, dealing with conflicts requires a willingness to learn new, non-abusive approaches to conflict resolution.

In this chapter, you will read about starting new relationships and how to develop equal or egalitarian relationships. We will examine some of the areas that couples frequently have conflicts about and explore how violence influences these conflicts and how to deal with them in a mutually respectful manner.

In the following story, Elliot explains how his attitudes about women had an impact on how he responded to his partner when they had conflicts.

Elliot's Story

Elliot grew up in a rural community in Iowa. His father was a strict disciplinarian and Elliot and his brothers tried hard not to cross him. Elliot's father was never violent with his mother.

Elliot was married to his wife Claudia for 17 years. When he came into our program, he only wanted to focus on the situations when Claudia was abusive, allowing him to feel justified in his use of violence. Elliot sees his life and his destructive relationship with Claudia differently today.

I grew up with the belief that a woman basically had to know her place. The family was an important unit, and traditional values dictated that the man commanded the respect of his family.

My childhood was rather lousy. Dad's values were such that everyone in the family was to work hard like he did, so there was little time for fun. All I ever did was work. I had very few dates with girls in high school because my parents didn't allow dating. That was the early sixties and I guess that's the way things were.

As soon as I graduated, I left home and went to college in Minnesota. All that pent-up frustration came out because I partied constantly. I started drinking a lot and that's when I began fighting. I got kicked out of college and joined the Air Force and ended up in Vietnam.

My self-esteem was very low. My father put me down a lot. He'd say I was no good and that I would never amount to anything. I think part of my experience in Vietnam reflected the suicidal tendencies that I had. I was depressed when I went into the service. Hell, I even volunteered for "door duty" on helicopters because the job was extremely dangerous. I never sought help for my depression and just dealt with all my feelings with the bottle.

When I got out of the service, I started hanging around a group of people who drank and got into trouble. I was working in construction at the time. My attitudes about women weren't very good. Basically, I felt women were there to be used. My thinking was that if they didn't want to play the game, then they could hit the road—there were plenty of other women. While I was emotionally and psychologically abusive, at this point I had not been violent with women.

I married Claudia in the early 1970s. We were married for 17 years and were in constant conflict from the very beginning. I never hit her while we were dating. Both of us were drinking quite heavily. Both of us wanted things our own way, so our relationship was a constant power struggle.

I think I wanted to replicate what I knew from growing up. I wanted the kind of relationship my father had with my mother, although I wasn't conscious of that at the time. I wanted to be in control and call the shots. Claudia resisted me, of course.

The first time I hit her was when she accused me of looking at other women. She started screaming at me in the car and the argument spilled over into the house, and that's when she slapped me and I hit her back. Whenever she hit me, it gave me a license to hit her back.

I have bad memories about my violence, her violence, and our mutual violence. The way she would start the violence was usually by slapping me. And then I'd slap her back. I never punched her, because of our size difference; I'm sure I would have killed her. The way I would start was by picking her up and throwing her on the couch, bed, or floor.

Sometimes when I thought that I was losing a verbal battle, I would pick her up and spank her on the bottom like a child. She was so much smaller than me that I could just hold her between my arm and body and spank her.

I specifically remember one incident when we were in Hawaii on vacation. We were arguing and she hit me several times and then kicked me in the groin. I came up swinging and grabbed her by the hair and slapped her several times. We physically fought for hours.

One time, we were having an argument and I was holding our son and she tried to kick me. She was going to try to kick me again so I started to leave and slammed the steel door. She put her arm out to stop me and her arm got crushed. I didn't intentionally try to hurt her, it was just a result of our violence. I took her to the hospital and she had some tendon damage.

There was another occasion that I took her to the hospital, but I was so drunk that I don't remember what happened, only that she had a head injury after I threw her. I thought the hospital officials were going to call the police because I told them what I had done, but they didn't. When they released her, we drove home and that was the end of it for then.

I controlled Claudia in many ways. I was the breadwinner and she wasn't working, so she had to come to me for money. That was a powerful tool because she would feel humiliated having to ask me for money. I'm sure I withheld money as a punishment.

I could intimidate her easily. I would hold my fist up and threaten to beat her up. When she was sober she would cower, thinking I would punch her. If she was drinking, my intimidation didn't seem to scare her.

I would call her a bitch because she hated that. I would compare her to other women as a way to put her down. I'd imply that she wasn't living up to my standards.

My son saw a lot of the violence. When he was around I would try to do or say things that would indicate that the violence was his mother's fault.

On a couple of occasions, I would take a gun from the house and leave, hoping that she would see that she had pushed me too far. I wanted her to think that I might kill myself. Well apparently she did, because she called the police and they took all of my guns.

When I first came into the Domestic Abuse Intervention Project, I couldn't seem to focus on me, it was always her. I quit the program and went into alcohol treatment. I then came back into the program because I wanted the violence to stop and to get a handle on my life. I realized by that time, however, that my relationship was not going to work.

I'm in a new relationship now and have been married for two years. I don't have the desire or the need to control. I know who I am. I don't need to control her to feel good and I don't desire the power that I sought with Claudia. I don't need to win when we have disputes or conflicts.

The most important thing that happened to me in this program was that people listened to me and didn't call me a no-good son-of-a-bitch. It was the first time that people seemed to care. The counselors told me that I had a life to lead and that I could make changes. It was a revelation.

I try and apply some of the tools that I learned in the program. I take time-outs and try and use self-talk when I feel myself reverting to old patterns. I'm much more aware of my feelings.

My new partner and I make decisions together, although I guess I still see myself as head of the household. I think it's more of a perception than reality. I guess there's still some male stuff I need to look at—like when we get into the car, I drive.

I still meet with some of the men from my group to continue focusing on issues that I need to work on. I've come a long way and I feel good about that.

Elliot describes his relationship with Claudia as a constant power struggle. Many forces kept them in this destructive and unhappy relationship. Elliot's belief that he is the head of the household in his new relationship points to a belief that he holds on to about the roles of men and women, despite the groups and programs he has been through. However, he maintains that his life is different today and that his change is an on-going process.

New Relationships, Old Problems

Elliot made a decision not to get involved with someone immediately after the break-up of his marriage. He wanted to work through some of his problems. Many men, however, get into a "rebound relationship"—they become involved with someone else right away. This way they do not have to experience the pain and grief of losing a relationship or confront the hurt they caused their previous partner.

In our groups, a man in a rebound relationship will report how everything is great with this new woman and how different she is from the partner he just left. He explains how this person does not have the same problems and defects that he believes his former partner had. This is a common trick of denial. Comparing his past relationship with his present one allows him to subtly justify his past abusive behavior.

However, when men jump into rebound relationships, they usually do not take the time to sort out the mistakes of the past. Because they are not experiencing major conflicts in their new relationship they do not believe they need to make changes. In the early stages of the relationship the man and his new partner are usually on their best behavior. When people are dating, they often try not to reveal flaws and overlook character deficiencies because they want the relationship to work.

The problem for a man who has battered is that he often reverts to familiar ground. He finds someone he really likes and immediately wants to possess and control her. When she resists, he uses what has worked before—threats, intimidation, and violence—to get what he wants. Ultimately, the cycle of violence begins all over again.

If your relationship has ended, take some time before you get involved with someone else. It is important to work on the issues that led to your violence before entering into a new relationship.

As Anthony explains below, giving yourself time to sort things out can have positive results. You do not have to wait for a new relationship as long as he did, but the point he makes is clear.

"I thought about getting involved after Vickie and I split," said Anthony. "I certainly had a lot of opportunities, but I had been violent with two women and didn't want to do it again. I kept going to the group. Then I went to a support group so I could continue to work on my issues. It was five years before I really believed I had come to terms with all this stuff. I'm now in a real good relationship and I'm glad I waited."

Participating in counseling or a domestic violence group can be helpful. You do not have to attend many sessions, and going does not mean there is something psychologically wrong with you. A few sessions where you are honest can be valuable and you may get the kind of feedback you need. The sessions can provide insight about what you need to change and work on.

Sorting out your prior response to conflicts and clarifying

the beliefs you had about women and relationships will help you know what to be aware of in the future. If someone videotaped an argument you had with your partner and played it for you, I am sure you could pick out precisely where you made mistakes and how you could handle the situation differently now. This is the kind of feedback and insight counseling and support groups can give you.

Here are some issues and techniques you may still need to work on:

- confronting your possessiveness and jealousy

- letting go of always being right and having things your way

- trying to be less critical

- finding ways of being more intimate

- practicing communication and negotiation techniques

For some, the thought of living alone is scary. However, living alone does not mean that you have to be lonely. Meeting new people, connecting with old friends, and finding activities of interest in your community can enrich your life. You could choose to live with friends or find a roommate, if your finances require it. The important thing is to *take your time* before entering a new relationship. Work on your problems and make sure you are confident that in your new relationship you will remain non-abusive.

Egalitarian Relationships

In egalitarian, or equal, relationships, couples work through traditional gender expectations. Often, people who have been in relationships where there were bitter and divisive struggles around gender roles and equality want new role definitions and a more free and healthy interchange with their partner.

Women who previously were in traditional relationships may now seek something different. They are often quite clear about what they expect and what they are willing to accept in a new relationship. Similarly, a new consciousness is emerging in a growing number of men. They see egalitarian relationships with women as a path to liberation rather than as the loss of control.

What do I mean by "liberation" for men? Here are some examples. Egalitarian relationships permit men to go beyond feeling *obliged* to share in child care; they may *desire* the responsibilities of shared parenting and the rewards of being involved fathers. In egalitarian relationships, men *encourage and support* partners who are pursuing new careers and community involvement. These men are likely to feel less threatened by their partner's aspirations, because they see that mutual development, growth, and support from each other enhance the partnership.

Such relationships were not common in my youth, and I suspect this was true for many of my generation (the baby boomers). My mother fulfilled the traditional female role. When she did enter the job market, her position with my father changed because she became less dependent.

Men in our groups frequently say that they have equal relationships. But as we begin to discuss roles and household responsibilities, a different picture emerges, as is shown in the following exchange.

Michael: Lloyd, you say that you and Patty have an equal relationship. Tell us how that works.

Lloyd: Well, I think it's pretty equal. I do a lot of the yard work and stuff with the car and she does most of the housework.

Michael: So you mow the yard once a week and she does the cleaning, cooking, and child care.

Lloyd: It's not like I'm forcing her to do this stuff, but she's better at a lot of it. Look, I've tried to help out when she asks, but she's never satisfied with the way I do it. I mean, she doesn't like the way I fold the towels—you know they have to be folded into three perfect sections . . . so she doesn't want me to do the laundry. And let's face it, most women can cook better than men, so she does it. With child care—well, after all, she is the mother. It's not like I don't help out, but there are certain things that she can do better than me and certain things that I can do better than her.

Some of Lloyd's explanation may be accurate. Patty may want to assert control over the household areas she feels are her domain. When a person does not have much power or many options, that person will want to hold on to areas in which she has some control. In other words, your partner looks for a niche to call her own.

Some men in our groups have admitted that they do a sloppy job folding laundry, cleaning, or cooking on purpose so their partners will perceive them as incapable of doing these chores. Pretending incompetence is an old childhood strategy that worked while growing up, so many men think, why not use it now? Television shows and movies constantly reinforce the image of the incompetent male in the household. Living up to those limited expectations allows men to avoid responsibilities.

Yet today many men realize the importance of equal partnership. They have examined failed relationships and see how their definitions of roles for men and women became obstacles. In these past relationships, struggles and conflict over unfair role definitions and work distribution took the place of friendship and intimacy.

Because egalitarian relationships are new territories, you may stumble and experience confusion. A commitment to making the relationship work and communicating expectations and needs are critical for success. We have all the tools we need to make an equal partnership work; we just need to use them.

The Equality Wheel (see page 136) was developed by the Duluth Domestic Abuse Intervention Project. (14) (If you have difficulty reading the wheel, see the text reproduced in the Appendix.) As you can see, there are many elements to an equal

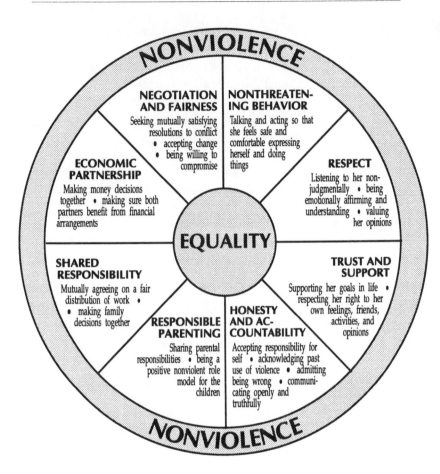

The wheel shows the following segments around the central hub labeled **EQUALITY**, with **NONVIOLENCE** circling the outer rim:

NEGOTIATION AND FAIRNESS
Seeking mutually satisfying resolutions to conflict • accepting change • being willing to compromise

NONTHREATENING BEHAVIOR
Talking and acting so that she feels safe and comfortable expressing herself and doing things

ECONOMIC PARTNERSHIP
Making money decisions together • making sure both partners benefit from financial arrangements

RESPECT
Listening to her nonjudgmentally • being emotionally affirming and understanding • valuing her opinions

SHARED RESPONSIBILITY
Mutually agreeing on a fair distribution of work • making family decisions together

TRUST AND SUPPORT
Supporting her goals in life • respecting her right to her own feelings, friends, activities, and opinions

RESPONSIBLE PARENTING
Sharing parental responsibilities • being a positive nonviolent role model for the children

HONESTY AND ACCOUNTABILITY
Accepting responsibility for self • acknowledging past use of violence • admitting being wrong • communicating openly and truthfully

relationship. Consider this wheel from time to time. Are you relating to your partner in a manner that reflects the positive elements of the wheel? If not, review the Negotiating Guide on page 151, and practice some of the exercises in this book, especially "Negotiating Roles" which follows later in this chapter, to get back on track.

Sharing the Load

While society has changed considerably in the last generation, the division of labor in many homes has not. The majority of families today cannot make it financially on one income, and both men and women must work. Yet women still clean, cook the meals, do the laundry, and provide most of the child care. Arguments often occur when women express resentment about this unequal—and unfair—load.

Men who think that taking out the trash and occasionally doing the dishes are the only household responsibilities they need to fill are being unfair. Yet in our groups these men often describe their partners as "nags" who are always "bitching." In one group, Herman discussed an argument that he and his partner Roberta had.

Herman: This woman is really something, man. I mean, last week, almost every day she was ragging on me. She says I don't help out enough. I swear, it's like living with my mother sometimes.

Michael: Two things before we proceed. Does "this woman" have a name?

Herman: Yeah, Roberta is her name.

Michael: This word ragging. I hear men use the word a lot. Men often say that if a woman is upset she must be "on the rag," or "it must be that time of the month." To me that term is used to belittle women's anger and is a derogatory statement about a woman's menstrual cycle.

Herman: Shit, it's getting to the point where you can't say anything anymore. Okay, how about if I say she was nagging?

Michael: Would you ever say a man was nagging?

Herman: Let's just say she was in my face.

Michael: Okay. So she was in your face because she feels you aren't doing enough around your home. Is there any truth to what she is saying?

Herman: Ever since she went from part-time to full-time at the hotel where she works, she expects me to do all this extra stuff at home. I work hard all day. I know she works hard too, but cleaning rooms isn't as stressful as a steelworker's job.

Michael: So even though she's working full-time, you expect her to do all the household stuff too?

Herman: You're starting to sound like her. Look, if she asks me to do something, I do it.

Michael: It's pretty obvious you are going to continue to have conflicts around this Herman. I mean if she has to ask you to do your part, I'm sure she'll be resentful. Is there any way you can sit down with her and figure out a plan? You know, kind of divide up the responsibilities?

After a lengthy discussion, Herman admitted that the position he was taking wasn't fair. He agreed to sit down with Roberta and work out something where they would share the load.

When we speak about sharing the load in an egalitarian relationship, we are not talking about something like cutting an apple in half, everything fifty-fifty. Some people think that equality means you do the dishes one night and I'll do them the next night; you clean the house this week and I'll do it next week; you bring the kids to soccer this month and I'll do it next month; we switch off on paying bills and going grocery shopping . . . . Egalitarian relationships do not have to be that rigid.

The following exercise will help you understand how to share responsibilities in a relationship. If your relationship has ended or is ending, the exercise may still be worthwhile. Use it to review your past relationship. You may develop some insight that will be helpful in future relationships.

Exercise: Negotiating Roles With your partner, make a list of your joint and separate responsibilities and obligations:

_____

_____

_____

_____

_____

Now write down who always, or for the most part,

a. pays the bills

b. cooks the meals

c. buys groceries

d. buys the children's clothes

e. feeds the children

f. cleans the home

g. repairs things

h. washes and folds the laundry

i. takes care of the car

j. handles social contacts

k. other _____

_____

_____

The purpose of this exercise is not to judge, but rather to assess who does what in the relationship. Use this list to figure out together the responsibilities you and your partner need to modify so that the relationship is more equal.

Often, couples get into ruts regarding responsibilities, but do not express their displeasure to each other. Consequently, resentment grows. If these feelings are not communicated, your resentment tends to spill out during other disagreements. So it is better to deal with this issue directly, clearly, and fairly.

As you and your partner complete the above exercise, you may find that sub-issues come up under each category. Each of these should be dealt with. One partner may also try to hold on to certain responsibilities for reasons of their own. For example, parents often disagree about disciplining children, school grades, setting boundaries and curfews, and values involving parental decision making. If one partner holds on to a major share of responsibility for the children in order to influence these decisions, this needs to be addressed as well.

Whether you and your partner have lived together for years or for months, take time periodically to make a list of your joint responsibilities. Talking about and modifying these responsibilities can be an important and perhaps relationship-saving exercise. By looking at each others' needs and listening to each others' concerns, you pave the way for healthy future negotiations about problems and issues that have not yet surfaced. You may have to reevaluate the way you share responsibilities, but you will find the journey to true partnership that much more rewarding.

The Issue of Money

Someone once said that money is the root of all evil. Money causes people to react in strange ways. Nations go to war over it and individuals go to jail trying to steal it. We work the majority of our lives to earn enough of it to survive—and couples often disagree about it.

We live in a money-driven, market-oriented society in which most of us need money for the necessities of life, and most of us do not have enough. The pressure to make money to live affects everyone. So, of course, it is a source of stress and conflict in even the healthiest relationships.

Our views about money are shaped by our upbringing. If you grew up in a household with limited resources, that is likely to have an impact on how you deal with money. If you saw your parents scrimp to get by, you might mirror that experience. Or you might try to do the opposite even if you do not have the resources. If yours was a family of means, you may have received very different messages, which will undoubtedly affect your attitudes about spending and saving.

When I grew up in the 1950s and 1960s, my parents went from having nothing to reaching middle class, the American dream. Even though our family had greater opportunities than some families today, my mother always reminded us children of how hard my father worked for every dollar when we received our weekly allowance. When I became an adult, I adopted an attitude of "you can't take it with you," partly in response to my parents' worrying and my own feelings of guilt. Yet, as much as I tried to get away from my upbringing, my parents' voices still echoed in my mind. Consequently, at different times in my adult life, I have been overly concerned about not having enough money or dwelt on financial problems.

When you enter into a relationship with someone, you have to combine both of your ideas about spending and saving. If your priorities and values are different, conflicts occur. In some traditional relationships, men believe that all the decisions about spending money should be made by them. Even in relationships where the woman also works, the man may assume decision-making responsibility because of this belief, and because money is power. Controlling the money usually gives a person more authority in the relationship.

Control over money is a prominent factor in battering as well. Victims of domestic abuse often report that, besides the fear of threatened violence, what kept them locked in an abusive relationship was their lack of financial resources.

In one of our groups, Frank related the following story about money.

"When we got married, there really wasn't any discussion about money," he said. "Jackie wasn't working at the time, so I obviously was supporting the family. I would give Jackie some cash every week to buy groceries and have some spending money. When she went back to work and started making her own money, we had all kinds of disagreements because she felt she should be able to spend her paycheck any way she wanted. She wasn't making very much, but I thought her pay and mine should be put together. I guess I was suspicious of what she was doing with the additional money, because I started accusing her of having affairs and plotting to leave me. That's when the physical violence got pretty bad. Jackie got a protection order and is seeking a divorce."

The experience of Frank and Jackie is not unusual. During our group session, it took a long time for Frank to understand how humiliating and dependent Jackie felt because she had to ask for a few extra dollars to buy herself or the children something. Though he finally acknowledged how Jackie may have felt, Frank refused to yield on what he believed was a fairness question, making statements like, "Women are just out to screw men." His hurt and anger about Jackie leaving him kept him from seeing how his violence affected her and how he used money to control her.

When the discussion of economic control comes up in our groups, men frequently say that they "give" their paychecks to their partners, so women really have financial control. When group members discuss disagreements they have had over money, the examples are similar to the experience Rick explained in group.

Michael: Rick, you were talking about an argument you had with Angie last week about money. You said that you think she is always blaming you for the amount of debt you both carry. Do you think she is really blaming you, or is it just that she is concerned over your financial situation?

Rick: I understand her concern and I realize she wants to get a handle on our expenses. I mean, I don't like to be in debt either. But I do feel that she uses a very blaming tone when she brings up examples of things we didn't need to spend money on.

Michael: Why do you say that?

Rick: Well, she usually mentions the things that *I've* bought, or that *my* priorities aren't right. Like she will say that we shouldn't have gotten the motor for the boat, even though she knows how much I like to fish, and that I charged a bunch of tools at Sears that we're still paying for. Yeah, I think she brings these things up in a blaming way when we get into it.

Michael: You said earlier that you understood her concerns and that you also have concerns about your debt. Can you see any way that you could resolve this?

Rick: I don't know. It seems that whenever we talk about it, we usually end up fighting.

The issue of money in relationships is complex and difficult for couples to sort out. Sometimes, trust issues that get raised call the entire relationship into question. When two people become a couple, do their funds become one? If one person makes more money is that person entitled to a greater say in how it is spent? Who gets to decide?

There is no one set of rules to follow when dealing with money issues. Couples have to sit down and decide what feels fair to them. Both people must take into consideration the forces that shape their partner's opinions and beliefs, and their own. The goal should be a compromise. Remember that one aspect of partnership is a commitment to sort through the tough decisions in a respectful and fair way

Exercise: Handling Money Problems If you get stuck in a money conflict, try the following exercise. You can either think about your answers or write them in a notebook or journal.

1. Describe clearly, simply, and as fairly as you can the money problem you are having.

_____

_____

_____

2. What do you think your partner's perception of the problem is?

_____

_____

_____

3. When and where do you and your partner usually argue about this issue? e.g., What time of the week, day, or month. Do you argue on the phone, at home, in public?

_____

_____

_____

4. Do you think it is possible to reach a compromise that works for both of you? Yes ____ No ____ Maybe ____

5. If yes or maybe, what can you do to safely initiate a discussion where you and your partner negotiate a solution to this conflict? (Safely means without controlling, provoking, or blaming.)

6. If no, what can you do to handle this conflict safely over the long term?

_____

_____

_____

Following are the answers given by Erwin in one of our groups.

1. Describe the problem:

   I think she is too uptight about money and blames me for us being in debt.

2. What do you think her perception of the problem is?

   She thinks I'm not concerned enough about our financial problems and that I'm willing to spend money we don't have.

3. When and where do we argue about this issue?

   Usually at the end of the month when the bills are to be paid.

4. Can a compromise be worked out?

   Maybe.

5. If yes or maybe, how can you safely negotiate a solution?

   (The group helped Erwin with some possible solutions)

   a. Discuss budgets and money commitments at the beginning of the month rather than when the bills are due and both people are anxious.

   b. Discuss major projects or purchases that may need to be made during the year and attempt to reach agreement on priority items.

   c. See a financial counselor.

The issues surrounding money don't have to be as complicated as you make them if you can come to a cooperative arrangement. There has to be give-and-take and a willingness to compromise. Most of us have money problems at some time in our lives. For many, living from paycheck to paycheck is a reality. Still others are unemployed or underemployed, and have limited resources. Regardless of your economic struggle, working together with your partner to make ends meet is far more preferable—and successful—than working against each other.

Expressing Feelings

I remember observing a men's group and noticing a chart on the wall called a "feelings" chart. On it were named about a hundred different feelings. The group leaders said they used the chart because the men in the group had a hard time identifying what they were feeling. I thought, so it's come to this—we can't tell anybody how we feel and we need a chart?

I think as men we know exactly how we feel. There may be many feelings going on at one time, which causes confusion, but we know what we are feeling. Most of us don't like to talk about or acknowledge what we are feeling because it makes us vulnerable. And, as we discussed in Chapter 1, vulnerability in men is considered a sign of weakness.

The following discussion took place in one of our groups.

Dan: Barbara asks me questions sometimes about our relationship and I just kind of freeze. My responses are usually vague. I know she wants me to say more because she keeps asking me questions and seems frustrated. She says we don't communicate.

Michael: This seems to be a common theme. Why is it so hard for men to communicate?

Lance: I think that it's upbringing. When I think of the way we played, us boys as compared to my sisters, it was totally different. My sisters would talk and talk about their friends. They would be real upset if they got into arguments. I could never understand how they put so much time and effort into sorting things out in their relationships with other girls. For us guys, hell, if you got into a fight with another guy, you just said 'Fuck him' and moved on with your life.

Michael: That's kind of sad, isn't it? Do you think that upbringing stuff has an impact on our relationships today?

Dan: It's partly upbringing. Barb always wants me to go deeper with my feelings. I don't know if I'm afraid to go deeper on an emotional level or I'm afraid to be that vulnerable, especially with a woman.

Michael: You think you will be hurt?

Dan: Maybe. I just wouldn't know where to start or how to do it.

Frank: I think part of it is that you don't want to hurt her. You know, I wasn't very happy in our relationship but was hanging in there for the kids and stuff. If I was really honest, I'd hurt her. I think men can express themselves but choose not to.

Michael: Do other men think that males choose not to share feelings?

Frank: I can't speak for all men, but I think they do. I know in past relationships I would purposely not talk to her, to keep her guessing.

Michael: Keep her guessing?

Frank: Sure. She never knew what I was thinking about her or the relationship. I always had the upper hand. Kind of a control thing.

We see that the reasons why men don't express their feelings are varied. For some men it is a fear of vulnerability, for others it is a tactic to control their partners, as Frank did.

Many men express feelings after committing a violent act. Some cry and ask for forgiveness. This expression of remorse or shame is often sincere. At other times it is simply another tactic to relieve personal responsibility for the violence, or to calm her anger.

Men in our society are conditioned not to express feelings or cry. Most men can remember a childhood experience when they were told, "Stop crying, be a man!" The problem is, the more men repress their inner feelings, the more difficulty they have expressing themselves in intimate relationships.

In one of our groups, Carlos talked about a painful childhood memory.

Carlos: I remember coming home from school one day feeling like shit because some of the kids were picking on me and I had started to cry. I must of have been about seven or eight. I mean, this was big-time humiliation. I went home and my parents knew something was wrong, so I told them what happened. My dad just said that I shouldn't take any crap from them and now it's only going to get worse because I showed them I was weak. My mom wasn't much better. She said she'd call the school if it happened again.

MaryAnn: What did you *want* them to say?

Carlos: I just wish they would have acknowledged what I was going through—you know, just let me know that they understood.

MaryAnn: What would have happened if they had asked you how you felt?

Carlos: My parents weren't like that with me and my brothers. You know, they had the idea that it's a rough world out there and you gotta be tough. I think they meant well, but I'll never forget how alone I was with all that stuff.

Most men could relate similar boyhood experiences of being all alone with their feelings. In most homes with fathers, Dad takes the detached role, believing he is providing good modeling for his sons. Would it have been so difficult for Carlos' parents to ask, "How do you feel about it?" or "I bet you feel pretty lousy, don't you?" It would have been much better for Carlos if his parents had acknowledged his feelings, or at least let him know that he was understood.

Parents usually do what they think is right. They prepare boys to become men—but what are the criteria for becoming a man? "You have to be ready to compete, because it's a dog-eat-dog world out there." "You have to be ready to kill, because your country may call you to fight in war." "You have to be ready to win, because men are failures if they lose." "You have to be in control, because men are supposed to be powerful." These messages leave little room for emotions and feelings that aren't tied to winning, fighting, and being in control.

The problem is that the feelings men experience do not go away just because they are not given permission to express them. We repress them for our own survival, but they do not go away. The explosiveness of men's anger (a feeling generally allowed and understood) is usually primed by their many submerged feelings, but what we mostly see is just the anger. Many men use alcohol or drugs to mask or numb the other feelings, but the numbness is usually temporary.

As Bernice states, you never know what to expect with a man who holds his feelings back and then explodes.

"Living with my partner was like living under siege," she said. "He would beat me up about once a month. It was almost like things would build and build within him. He usually wouldn't tell me what was going on inside. But I could almost predict when all this rage would build and culminate in him battering me."

What should men do with the feelings they experience? What do you do when you feel insecure, overwhelmed, scared, sad, or unhappy? Men need to find appropriate and positive ways of expressing these feeling to friends and family members, as well as to their partners. Perhaps they should start by talking. They may not release all their pent up emotion by talking, but at least they will not feel so alone.

One caution: If you are still in the relationship with the woman you abused, you need to exercise control over how and when you express your feelings. Your partner may still be afraid of you and may not understand how you have changed.

Can your expression of feelings be counterproductive for the relationship? There is a distinct difference between honestly talking about what is going on in your life and using your feelings to manipulate or control your partner. For instance, talking about how you *feel* jealous or *feel* insecure about your partner going out with a friend in order to keep her from going is controlling. Though you should be able to talk to her about these feelings, if your intent is to make her feel guilty and not go, you are indirectly imposing your will on her.

Repressing your feelings and thoughts is also unfair to your partner, as she does not get to know the real you. As your current relationship gets healthier, or in your new relationship, you will need to make decisions about your level of intimacy. Being in touch with your own feelings and caring about your partner's feelings is an important part of this. There is an element of risk, because intimacy requires a certain level of vulnerability. This is not easy for men.

You may think that not showing emotion or talking about your feelings makes you stronger or in control, but in the long run it affects your mental health and increases the possibility of explosive outbursts. We all have fears, experience pain, get frustrated, or feel insecure. Denying your feelings robs you of totally experiencing all that life has to offer—the good *and* the bad, the pain *and* the joy.

Learning to Negotiate and Compromise

How do we settle conflicts? For thousands of years world leaders, mediators, counselors, and peacemakers have grappled with difficult issues and tried to reconcile opposing views. From children on the playground to presidents of great countries, we argue, debate, quarrel, and fight. We will always have disagreement and conflict in relationships, yet conflict does not have to be hurtful and individuals certainly do not have to resort to abusive behavior to make their point.

A fair way to resolve conflicts in a relationship is to agree on guidelines for discussing difficult issues. For men who have been violent in the past, this is crucial. Following is a fifteen-point guide you and your partner can use to help you resolve conflicts and problems fairly and respectfully.

The Negotiation Guide

1. Regardless of how angry or hurt I feel I will remain nonviolent.

2. If I disagree with my partner's position I will still be respectful toward her.

3. I will remain seated during the discussion.

4. I will not yell, scream, or use my voice in an intimidating manner.

5. I will not threaten my partner in any way.

6. I will not use put-downs, call my partner names, or be sarcastic or belittling.

7. I will not bring up past incidents to prove a point.

8. I will avoid blaming or shaming statements.

9. I will strive not to get defensive.

10. I will listen to my partner's position and refrain from interrupting.

11. I will commit to work toward a compromise.

12. I will be willing to explore my own issues and take responsibility for mistakes I have made.

13. I will respect my partner's wishes to end the discussion.

14. I will be honest.

15. I will talk about my feelings but will not use them as a way to manipulate my partner.

Couples have spontaneous disagreements in restaurants and movie theaters or at the homes of friends and family. It is better not to try and resolve conflicts over difficult issues in public because you cannot talk frankly, it is often embarrassing, and you may find yourself disregarding the Negotiation Guide for arguing fairly.

Before discussing the issues you disagree about, both of you should agree on a good time to work on the problem. Make sure you have enough private time without interruptions from kids, business, or phones. One of you should state your position without being interrupted, regardless of how long it takes. When that person is finished, the other starts. Remember the Negotiation Guide!

After you have both had an opportunity to talk about your position, try and see where you are in *agreement*. Are the areas of disagreement significant or can you find a way to compromise? Remember, if you are stuck there is nothing wrong with seeking assistance from a counselor in your community.

Some disagreements can be resolved quickly; others are more complicated and may involve painful issues. Not talking about these problems is *not* the solution. You may not resolve the issue that day or that night, but you can begin the work.

If you are still in a relationship with a woman you have abused, she may not want to work on the same issues as you do. Her trust in you may be diminished. She may still harbor anger and resentment because of the abuse, and may be confused about her feelings. The following discussion occurred in one of our groups.

Bob: I don't get it. Jessie always wanted me to talk more with her, you know, talk about my feelings. Well, now when I want to, she either doesn't want to or gets pissed.

Michael: What do you do?

Bob: Nothing, I let it go. But I'm getting frustrated. I mean, I feel like I'm making changes and I want to work on our relationship, and she's resisting.

Michael: You know, Bob, you really need to give Jessie time. After all that's gone on you can't just expect her to adapt to your agenda. Sometimes when people heal, they get in touch with a lot of feelings, including anger at the person who hurt them. You need to give her as much time as she needs.

Arguing fairly takes two people committed to working things out. Bob has been learning things in group and wants to work on the relationship. Jessie may or may not want to work things out, but she is clearly not ready. The Negotiation Guide may not work right now for women who have been battered.

Regardless of how your partner responds, you can still commit to the Negotiation Guide. Because of your past history of abuse it is important that you set high standards for yourself. If your partner says something hurtful or inappropriate during a discussion, it is not necessary for you to match her. Once you take that step, you begin the slide down that slippery slope to where you do not care what you say and do, and you may become abusive.

Settling differences requires three basic things:

1. The desire to listen to the other person.

2. The willingness to compromise.

3. The fortitude to work things out, regardless of how difficult the task.

Before we married, my partner and I could not seem to resolve certain fundamental issues regarding commitment to our relationship. We would argue, disagree, and could not come to a satisfactory resolution. So we decided to seek help and went to a therapist who had us do the following exercise.

Both of us were seated face to face. My partner was to start by stating her position on commitment to me. I was not to interrupt. When she was done, I was to repeat back what she had said, and then it would be my turn.

It seemed pretty simple, and I remember thinking, "Why are we paying $75.00 an hour for this?" However, I agreed, and my partner proceeded to tell her story, which took about ten minutes. The therapist asked me to repeat what my partner had said. Although she had just finished, I was astonished to find that I could not remember a single thing she had said! I was so angry, and concentrating so thoroughly on how I was going to counter all the things she had said, that I literally did not hear her.

That experience taught me a lot about listening. Sometimes we are so convinced of the correctness of our position that we build walls around ourselves. Or we may be hurt or offended by what the other person is saying and our response is to hurt back. Being able to listen to another person's feelings and thoughts on an issue is a skill worth possessing. It takes practice and determination.

On certain issues it may be difficult to compromise and reach a place where both people feel comfortable. Sometimes you may have to leave things alone for a while. And not everything is open to negotiation, as we see in the following group discussion.

MaryAnn: Art, you said last week that you had a disagreement with Ginny about going back to school. You said you worked out a compromise. What happened?

Art: Well, basically we agreed that she would wait until we were in better shape financially before she went to school.

MaryAnn: When will that be?

Art: As soon as I get the raise I've been promised. Maybe next year.

MaryAnn: And Ginny is okay with waiting? You said before that this has been a longstanding issue with the two of you, and that she really wanted to go back to school.

Art: I think she was disappointed, but after we discussed the pros and the cons, she basically agreed with my position that we couldn't afford it right now.

MaryAnn: So you're saying there were no alternatives like school loans?

Art: I don't want us going into that kind of debt. I mean, she doesn't even know what kind of degree she wants. She just wants to go back to school. There's no way that I want to be saddled with several thousands of dollars of school loans.

Art believes that he and Ginny have worked out a compromise, but in actuality he just put up a roadblock that was impossible for her to go around. He later admitted that there were other issues about her going back to school that disturbed him, but when confronted he would always bring it back to the money issue. He was convinced that he was being rational and that his position was right. However, the fact that Ginny accepted the money dilemma as a reason for their decision does not mean that a fair and mutual compromise had been worked out between them.

A major issue for couples often arises if one partner wants to make a change in his or her life. Changing jobs, going back to school, joining an organization, or pursuing new friends can become problem issues if one partner feels that the status quo of the relationship will be disturbed. Change can be scary. For men who have been violent and are still in the relationship with the partner they abused, the feelings about such change may be even more pronounced.

Many men in our groups talk about feeling insecure about their relationship. They acknowledge the pain they have caused, and wonder why their partner would want to stay with them. When their partner expresses an interest in doing something different, they become suspicious. They *want* to believe that they are entering into true negotiation over a change that affects both partners and the relationship but, instead of encouraging their partner's aspirations and supporting the change, they become manipulative and controlling. Obviously, for their partner it is one more indication that they are not ready to change.

Compromise does not mean that one party has to sacrifice or change to accommodate the other person's needs. If you follow the points in the Negotiation Guide you should be able to resolve conflicts in a respectful way that honors each partner's freedom to make decisions and takes into account the impact of these decisions upon the relationship.

Men who have been abusive in relationships are used to getting their way. Essentially, that is the *reason* for the violence and other abusive behavior. Much like an alcoholic living "one day at a time," you have to make a personal acknowledgment that you will not always get what you want, and a personal commitment to a partnership with someone who has an equal say in the relationship.

7

Healing

*Dave's Story — Support for Changing Men —
New Definitions of Masculinity — Health and
Balance — Dating: How Much of The Past Do We
Reveal? — Talking to Your Children about
Your Violence — Beyond Personal Change:
Educating the Community — Staying on Course:
Your Life-long Commitment — Conclusion*

In this chapter you will read about men changing, redefining masculinity, and getting and staying healthy on many levels. We will also examine issues related to staying accountable in relationships, talking with your children about your violence, and keeping your commitment to living a non-abusive and nonviolent lifestyle.

Dave's Story

Dave grew up in a violent home and was abusive in the majority of his relationships with women. After going through substance abuse counseling, he made a commitment to himself to get the help he needed to end the violence in his life and volunteered to participate in the Duluth Domestic Abuse Intervention Project. Dave now works with chemically dependent people and runs a group for abusive men.

The first time I saw someone getting hurt was my mom getting beat by my dad. He punched her in the head, kicked her, and pulled her across the floor by the hair. I was about five or six at the time.

There was a lot of violence in our house, which included uncles, aunts, and parents. Usually the violence occurred when people were drinking. I'm sure those early experiences shaped my thinking. It's strange, though, because although my brother saw all that stuff too, he never used violence. My parents' verbal message to us was not to be violent and to treat others with respect—especially your elders. Yet that's not what I saw growing up. We were told to never talk about the violence at home because it was a family matter.

My dad would whale on us kids. He worked for the railroad and he would often kick us with steel-toed boots. I remember him standing over me after beating me and saying, "I'll kill you, you little son-of-a-bitch." And I think the only reason he stopped was because he just got tired.

I always wanted to be accepted by my dad, but never was. Whenever my mother tried to stop him from beating us kids, she got beat. I remember sitting with her and both of us were crying. I asked, "Why can't we move out?" She said, "Things will be okay," but they never were okay. I've always been angry about my childhood.

My partner, Lori, and I grew up in the Duluth area, but we ended up in Chicago. I was 25 and she was only 15 when we moved in together. I was drinking a lot. Lori provided the things I needed—a clean house, someone to make my meals, and sex. While we had set up house, we weren't really that committed. I didn't want to get married to her, but the relationship was convenient.

The first time I hit Lori was when we first started dating. Even though we both had other relationships, I still saw Lori as mine. When I drank, I would end up fighting with men who were showing an interest in her.

I told Lori that I didn't want her friends coming over to the apartment unless I was there. The fact that other men were interested in her became an obsession with me. Sometimes I almost goaded her into telling me about her feelings toward other men. It didn't matter if what she said was right or wrong—it was always wrong.

It was almost a sadistic thing, like I was a military interrogator with a cigarette in his mouth asking these questions. With her being only 15, I was able to manipulate her with the questions. I would be in a good mood and ask her questions about men, and she would think it was okay to tell me about past relationships or men that she still found attractive. Then I would slap her. She would cry and not know what I was doing. I would hit her and apologize and then start the whole process over again. I must have slapped her at least two dozen times one night.

The abuse got worse. I moved from slaps to punches and even hit her in the stomach when she was pregnant. My violence included pulling her hair, pushing, and kicking her in the back when she was down. Early on I never hit her in the face because I didn't want to look bad to family and friends.

She knew I was a perfectionist and always kept the house perfect, even with three kids. And while she wasn't that beautiful, she had an incredible body. Sometimes I would look at her and think that this is someone I really want to be married to. Then there were other times when I would look at her and just glare.

I never trusted people, especially women. I always thought that women tried to get men to look at them or make a pass at them even if they were attached or married. I remember one time Lori was in this bowling league and she wanted to get a new outfit. I went with her to the store and helped her pick out this really sexy top. She had such a beautiful body, I told her how great she looked in it and that she should get it. Then eight hours later, I was saying, "You son-of-a-bitch, I saw the way you were crossing your legs." Then I accused her of wearing provocative clothes even though I had picked the clothes out.

Lori never really fought back, except sometimes she would kick at me when I had her down, and sometimes she would throw things at me. When that happened, then I would really nail her, usually using my fists, or I would kick her square in the ass. If she ran from me, I would kick her in the back.

I was always able to get Lori to forgive me. I guess I had a gift for talking, because I would always say things are going to be better and be real sensitive and then this smile would come on her face and she would say, "I know that wasn't really you."

When I look back on my violence today, I realize that I really wasn't out of control. I knew where to hit. I would usually avoid hitting her in the face. There were numerous times that I would have Lori pinned in a corner or be on top of her with my hand around her neck, yet I always knew when to stop. Often times, I would blame my violence on the alcohol. I would say things like, "You know what I'm like when I'm drunk."

Toward the end of the relationship, she would say things like, "Why don't you let me go home to my parents? You can see the kids anytime." When she talked like that I would get real nervous, because even though both of us were unhappy, I didn't want to be alone. I would promise her things, like we would get married.

The more I thought she was going to leave, the more controlling I became. I would check the phone bills to see how many calls she was making and to where. And then there was this neighbor friend of hers that I was real suspicious of, because I thought she was telling Lori things. I would tell Lori that I didn't want her to go over there anymore. If she was talking on the phone, I would stand in the doorway and glare at her or look at my watch and then interrogate her after she hung up.

I'd go up to her just like my dad did to us. I could scare the hell out of her. Actually, at that time, everyone was afraid of me because they had seen me going off on people, and as small as I was, I would beat the hell out of people. At home I would slam my fist on the table and there would be instant quiet. There was a certain feeling of power. I would just look and get what I wanted and I liked that. I got to watch any TV program I wanted. Lori was always trying to "keep the peace," just like my mom. She would always ask me what I wanted and I liked that feeling.

Of course, I was frequently emotionally abusive. I would call her a whore, slut, cunt, and a goddamn pig. I knew which words or put-downs hurt the most. The worst was calling her a goddamn pig. I would say, "Look at you, you goddamn pig, you ugly son-of-a-bitch, who the fuck would want you? Go look at yourself in the mirror!" She would start crying and say, "How can you say you love me and say these things to me?"

The worst incident that I remember was when we were living in the Twin Cities and the family was there—her mom and step-dad and my dad. I had been in a car accident several weeks before and my leg was in a cast. She had decided that she wanted to be away from me for a while. Anyway, I thought she was getting "smart" because her mom was there. When her family started to leave, I got up, grabbed Lori, and threw her down. I started whaling on her in the same way I would fight a man—ready to kill. I was on top of her, punching her everywhere about 20 times, until her dad managed to pull me off. That was probably the scariest incident. I knew, after that, that I needed to deal with my violence.

She finally left me and moved back to northern Minnesota. I moved to California. I would call her and ask her to come back to me. One time when I called, she hung up on me. That day I flew to Minnesota from San Francisco and slapped the hell out of her. The cops came and took me away, although I was never charged with anything.

In the late seventies, I came back to Minnesota. I was still drinking pretty heavy. I went out with two different women briefly. One I abused; the other I didn't. Then I entered treatment. I met Carol after treatment when I was getting my life together. I opened up a T.V. repair shop in a city outside of Duluth and we moved in together and things were going real well. I even told her about my past abuse.

I hit her once and she said if I ever did it again, she would get an order for protection. She had been battered before and made it clear to me that she wasn't going to put up with it again. Carol was afraid of me. I would drive the car real fast, which would scare her. She would be screaming "Stop the car!" But I wouldn't. Carol finally got an order for protection.

I started to go to these abuse groups partly because I wanted Carol to see that I was ready to make some changes. The longer I was in the program, the more I changed. My relationship with Carol ended, however.

I knew I had to make a lot of changes. I needed to let go of the jealousy. In my current relationship, I accept my partner having her own life and her own friends. I'm also more supportive of my partner and willing to listen to what she is saying, rather than just reacting.

Of course, quitting the alcohol and going through treatment forced me to look at myself. I've started to focus on my good qualities, my kindness, my ability to be gentle—things that women I dated said I possessed, but I never believed them.

I really feel okay with who I am. I've had to change the way I think about men and women. In the past, I believed that women were supposed to be submissive, and I would pick women who I knew wouldn't be resistant. My attitude toward women has changed.

I remember in group this counselor said, "If nothing changes, then nothing will change." It sounded strange, but it made sense to me, because I needed to change.

I've talked to all of my children about my alcoholism and violence. It's not easy to come face-to-face with the fact that they were afraid of me and that they did similar things that I did as a child, such as trying to stop their father from hitting their mother. I think it's important for former batterers to talk to their children. They all talk about how scary it was for them and how angry they were. It wasn't easy to talk to them about this stuff, but for me it's been important.

We go back in the past, not to relive the past, but to find out about the destructive patterns that still get in the way. I've told my present partner about my past. I still take time-outs from time to time. Once you've battered, you always have to be aware of who you are, where you've been, and what you are capable of doing.

I feel great about where I'm at today and the changes I've made. When I talk about my experiences today, I often say, "Once a batterer always a batterer." And I don't mean that in a negative way, like you can't change, but rather it's similar to being an alcoholic. I still read literature on alcoholism and attend AA, and I need to pay similar attention to the patterns I had developed around being controlling of women and how I handle conflict. The things I learned eight years ago—taking time-outs, sharing, letting go of the need to control, and being more accepting of who I am—are things I continue to work on.

If I let negative and destructive thoughts enter into my life, I think I have the potential to revert back. But I'm able to see the signs now. When a red flag or warning sign comes up, I know what to do and it's easier for me to recognize them.

The most rewarding thing now is for me to give back to others who are abusive what I've learned, and tell them how I've changed. It keeps me healthy. Change is a long process, but you can never stop.

Support for Changing Men

Struggling with the issues discussed in this book can be hard. Some men might claim that the analysis and self-reflection I ask of the reader only bring shame and guilt about one's maleness. The opposite is true. Awareness and understanding of sexism and the willingness to make changes are liberating.

Develop awareness by talking to people, both men and women, about the issues discussed in this book. In most communities, men, albeit in small numbers, are getting together to talk about masculinity, men's violence, and healing. Some men have joined men's organizations, like BrotherPeace and the National Organization of Men Against Sexism (NOMAS); or they work with women's organizations that confront sexism and violence against women in their community.

If you are a man committed to ending your own use of violence, attend a domestic violence program in your community. Go through the program for the information; you will also feel less isolated as you embark on a new path. Frequently, support groups are available after completing the program. I know many men who have built friendships with other men they met through these groups. Together, they continue to grapple with personal issues related to relationships and remaining non-abusive.

The process of change requires some men to give up certain friendships or activities, much like an alcoholic gives up a social situation where there is the temptation to drink. Going to a bar, party, or social function where other men tell sexist jokes or devalue women soon becomes objectionable to men trying to change their lives. You may want to confront these men, tell them that you do not appreciate their sexist comments, and try to educate them. Or you may decide that you want to be around more progressive men.

Several years ago, I was at a YMCA to play racquetball. After the game I was sitting in the sauna with about six or seven men and one of them began telling sexist jokes, to the delight of the others. When I said that I thought his jokes were sexist and insensitive, the sauna became uncomfortable. The man told me to "chill out," and said, "They're only jokes." Someone else said, "It's not like there's any women here to hear the jokes." I left wondering if I had overreacted. Then I thought, would I have been quiet if someone made a racist or anti-Semitic joke? What was the difference? And what difference did it make that there were no women there? Since I have recognized how destructive sexism is to women, I cannot remain silent. That does not mean I confront every man or woman who does or says something sexist. Confrontation can make people defensive or push them away. In a respectful way, I try to educate. I try to plant seeds. I know that I always run the risk of being rebuffed when I confront other men, but I also know that I may change some people along the way.

Like many of the men in this book, you probably will seek out friendships that are not superficial. Although there is nothing wrong with talking about sports or cars, there is more to life than box scores or overdrive transmissions. You will want relationships with men and women where you support each other's growth and change in a *true* spirit of friendship.

Men who are committed to change should not rely on women for all their support. They should make the changes for themselves. They should take responsibility and undo a system of violence that generations of men have constructed. Their rewards will be healthier relationships, children who value equality, and the knowledge that they are part of a revolutionary process that some day will bring about a more peaceful world.

New Definitions of Masculinity

Our masculinity is defined by our culture—whether we like it or not. The messages and expectations we are exposed to shape who we are.

For many men, the thought of being sensitive or caring is scary, as Ralph discussed in a group.

"After that last group, where we talked about what it meant to be a man, I really thought about all the comments that were made," he said. "Last weekend, I went down to the bar to watch the Vikings games. I watched the men around me. They all seemed lonely and content with their booze and football talk. I sat down with a few buddies and had a beer. We talked about the game and hunting. I tried to get them talking about some more personal things, but all that came out was Ben's divorce and how he thought he was getting screwed. Then we talked about who might make it into the play-offs."

This type of superficial conversation is typical of the patterns of "male bonding" men learn from childhood on. So-called "sensitive" boys are teased and ridiculed by their peers if they don't conform. This taunting emphasizes stereotypical male interests, and serves to keep us from developing complex self-images and forming deep relationships.

Look at these definitions of "man" in the *American Heritage Dictionary.* "MAN: 1. Any adult male human being, as distinguished from a female.... 5. A male human being endowed with such qualities as courage, strength, and fortitude, considered characteristic of manhood."

If courage, strength, and fortitude are the sole characteristics of manhood, that leaves no room for men to be compassionate, gentle, and nurturing. It is because of narrow stereotypes like this that men in growing numbers are seeking a healthier definition of masculinity, an emerging understanding that allows them, as men, to feel and give.

Allowing yourself to be sensitive and nurturing does not diminish your masculinity. Allowing yourself to feel makes you more human and compassionate. You become a better father, a closer partner, and a stronger friend. In fact, in many ways allowing yourself to feel helps you gain *greater* courage, strength, and fortitude.

The idea of changing can be frightening. It is much easier to stay the way we are. So many men in our groups are living unfulfilling lives, hurting others and themselves, and modeling a destructive path for their children. It does not have to be that way.

In my interview with Cassie, she said, "I think on some level my partner really wanted to change. He would tell me that he would get help but he wouldn't follow through. Things would go along pretty well and then something at work would happen and he would take it out on me. Because he never got any help, I don't think he saw any other way of living."

Some men are threatened when we talk about redefining masculinity. They are concerned about what they may have to change or give up. We discussed this issue in one of our groups.

Neil: I don't know if I believe that men need to change. I agree that we don't need to be so violent, but basically I like being a man.

Michael: I don't think that it's an issue of whether you like being a man or not. But I think there are ways that we get socialized that have a negative impact on how we live our lives. I mean why are we here?

Tom: We're here because the court said we had to be here.

Gordy: I know what he's saying and I agree to a point. We grow up in a culture where men are supposed to be a certain way. And I think violence is a big part of growing up male. I think, too, that controlling women is ingrained in us.

Michael: If what Gordy said is true, are there ways that we can redefine masculinity, keeping the positive stuff and throwing out those qualities that are destructive?

Gordy: I think we can. You know, I think back on my childhood and I feel bad. My father never said that he loved us kids, even though I know he did. He purposely was distant and never gave us approval. I almost think he was incapable of telling us.

Michael: That's sad.

Neil: Yeah, but fathers have to project that image of strength. I mean, I have a hard time saying that stuff to my kids. Just because I don't say it doesn't mean I don't have those feelings.

Michael: I think this discussion demonstrates the point I'm trying to make about how our culture defines masculinity. It also speaks to what we are losing as men, husbands, and fathers.

We should be proud to be men. Throughout history, there have always been men who have resisted the tide. Through deeds and words, Red Cloud, Martin Luther King, Jr., Tom Paine, Mahatma Gandhi, Chief Joseph, and Cesar Chavez have all fought against oppression and injustice. These men and countless others expressed profound sensitivity in their struggles. They had visions of a peaceful world where men and women were nurturing and shared a common dream for humanity.

Men *can* define masculinity for themselves. Our new definitions can include many important qualities. Within all men is the ability, and often the desire, to be sensitive and caring. Our loving inner self can emerge when we reject the notion that traditional male qualities are the only way of being masculine.

Health and Balance

I first learned about the idea of living in balance and harmony from a Native American man named Marlin Mousseau. Marlin grew up on the Pine Ridge Indian Reservation in South Dakota and now works with abusive men in Wisconsin. Marlin developed Project Medicine Wheel, a process designed to help abusive men in the Native American community understand their use of violence, motivate men to live in harmony and balance, and use traditional Indian ways for healing.

Marlin states that an individual is made up of four basic essences; emotion, body (the physical side), spirit, and mind (the intellectual side). If one of these areas is not functioning or is unhealthy, then the person is out of balance and is not living in harmony with the world. I think men are frequently out of balance. We, unfortunately, have little guidance or support to change our unhealthy lives.

The Emotional Side

Men in our groups often say that they do not know how to talk on a truly emotional level. This is because they have been socialized not to talk about their feelings. Gradually, they become afraid to show their true selves and their emotional side becomes disconnected from the whole. The longer men refrain from expressing their feelings the more difficult it becomes.

Occasionally, I have chosen to withdraw from my partner, hide my feelings, and not talk about what is going on in my life. Sometimes, I give her just a hint of what is going on or what may be disturbing me. Every time I hold back there is a consequence. I become more distant and our relationship suffers.

Men need to open up emotionally. We need to talk about what we are really feeling. Talking about emotions should not be limited to partners, but should be a precondition to new friendships with women and men. People usually *want* to talk about their lives on a less superficial level, but do not think they have permission. We feel that if we open up, our friends will think that there is something wrong with us, that we are too needy or self-absorbed. Talking on a deeper level takes practice and can never be a one-way street. You must genuinely care about what the other person is saying, thinking, and feeling, too. Your concern and response will be reciprocated. You do not need to solve each other's problems, just be there for each other.

The Physical Side

On the physical level, being active, staying in shape, and putting the right things into our bodies is necessary, but we often resist. Many people in the United States are out of shape, which is a harbinger of future physical problems. Men often ignore health problems and overwork themselves, thinking that they are invincible.

An exercise routine takes discipline. Exercise is not only good for the body, it is also emotionally uplifting. Yet there always seems to be something else to do or some reason not to exercise. There have been many times when I have left my workplace and felt that I had absolutely no energy to exercise. All I wanted to do was go home, watch the news, eat, and go to bed. I forced myself to go to the gym and, almost always, I enjoyed the exercise and felt reawakened and pleased that I had made the effort.

Balancing your physical side also requires monitoring what you put into your body. We hear how important it is to eat a healthy diet, change bad eating habits, and eat in moderation, yet we frequently ignore the advice. Men especially think that they can abuse their bodies and that nothing will happen. Many men think that cancer or heart disease will happen to someone else, or that there is always time to change. Some men continue to smoke despite the enormous medical evidence that tobacco use causes heart disease and cancer. They engage in unsafe sex even though they know the risks of AIDS and other diseases. They drink to excess and consume dangerous drugs regardless of the physical and psychological effects. Some men believe they are indestructible. This belief is illusory and dangerous. You can change this mistaken belief in immortality that men unfortunately hold: care about yourself.

If you are not involved in an exercise routine, commit to it now. Join a Y or an exercise club and find the routine that feels good and is fun. Buy some running shoes and power walk or jog. Play basketball, racquetball, or tennis. Lift weights, dance, or join an aerobics class. As the saying goes, Just Do It! At least three days of working out per week will keep your weight down, increase cardiovascular activity, and make you feel better.

The Spiritual Side

When I mention the spiritual level I am not referring to going to church or temple every weekend; that is your personal choice. What I am talking about is the need to get in touch with the world around you. This feeling of connectedness can occur in nature through meditating, walking in a park or in the woods, or sitting by a creek. Some people pray, chant, sing, or listen to music as a way of getting in touch with what is important about life. Everyone can find his or her own source of spiritual light.

Several years ago, I went to a retreat where I learned about meditation. We were asked to focus on the impermanence of life and the limited time we spend on the earth. I remember feeling quite sad during this meditation, a sadness that had much to do with my own inner feelings at the time. I was confused about the pain in the world and wondered about the purpose of my life. I had no answer. Today, when I think back on that time and the focus on impermanence, I realize the message. In the short time we are here, we need to live our lives with significance and purpose. We do not necessarily have to do something earth-shattering, just live with more compassion and love. It was an important lesson for me.

I forget that lesson a lot. I choose to live a spiritually unbalanced life because the world around me seems so cold, unloving, and angry. The collective pain of families and communities spills out all around me. I easily become withdrawn, and insulate myself by becoming cynical, self-absorbed, and uncaring. When the pain I see in my work overwhelms me, I know I am spiritually out of balance. Like most things in life, this is a choice. I can slow down, put my life in perspective, and take the necessary steps to reconnect with what is really important.

The Intellectual Side

On the intellectual level, men have been trained in particular ways. I think people often have a difficult time being open to new ideas. We get locked into thinking a certain way and refuse to hear opposing views. Listen, for example, to other men discuss politics. The debate takes on an almost war-like character with each person determined to win. I'm not suggesting that we be afraid to debate or give up some principled positions. But when we refuse to listen to other ideas, we become hardened.

You do not have to be a rocket scientist to nurture your intellectual side. Simply be open to information and ideas. Allow yourself time to reflect. To broaden your intellectual horizons, take a class, join an organization where ideas are shared, or volunteer in your community.

Unfortunately, television has become the dominant source of ideas and information for many people. While there is certainly entertainment value in television, too many individuals and families have become glued to their sets. TV sitcoms, movies, or sporting events often take priority over discussing ideas with family members or reading books.

Staying in balance is not easy. I am frequently aware of being out of balance. I remember going through a stressful time after I moved from Duluth to the Minneapolis/St. Paul area. I left a relatively small town, friends, and familiar territory for a large metropolitan city. I was emotionally drained. I lacked motivation and changed habits. I stopped exercising and became depressed. I finally went to a counselor to sort things out. On an emotional level, I needed to address my grieving about the move. On a physical level, I needed to develop a plan to take better care of myself, which included exercise, rest, and a good diet. Slowly, I worked my way through the depression.

Exercise: Health and Balance Awareness and the motivation to seek a healthier life are within your reach. The following exercise will help you to assess your present state and determine the steps you might want to take to live a life that is more in balance. You can either think about your answers or write them in a notebook or journal.

1. Think about or write how you feel about each level in your life today.

EMOTIONAL: _____

_____

_____

PHYSICAL: _____

_____

_____

SPIRITUAL: _____

_____

_____

INTELLECTUAL: _____

_____

_____

2. Think about or write some specific problems or deficiencies under each category (i.e., out of shape, hot-tempered, stuck, drinking too much, withdrawn, lacking purpose).

EMOTIONAL: _____

_____

_____

PHYSICAL: _____

_____

_____

SPIRITUAL: _____

_____

_____

INTELLECTUAL: _____

_____

_____

3. Think about or write some things you can do differently to bring these parts of your life more in balance.

EMOTIONAL: _____

_____

_____

PHYSICAL: _____

_____

_____

SPIRITUAL: _____

_____

_____

INTELLECTUAL: _____

_____

_____

Learn to recognize when you are out of balance and figure out ways to make healthy changes. Embarking on lifestyle changes is hard and the results are not instantaneous, but you *will* notice a difference. And it is worth it.

Dating: How Much of the Past Do We Reveal?

Many men do not tell a new partner of their past abuse. Although I understand the reasons for this reluctance, I think it is important to be honest in a new relationship. Telling your new partner about your past is a way of being accountable for your actions. Your new partner should have the right to confront you if she senses you are becoming abusive. She should have the right to insist that you make changes and/or seek help.

"When I told Lydia about my past, I was scared that she was going to run," Peter explained during a group meeting. "She seemed a little shocked at first, but I think she really trusted my commitment to being nonviolent. Once I made the decision to tell her, I knew I had to be totally honest about everything. Afterward, I felt incredibly free—as if a ball and chain had been removed from my leg."

Being honest about the past can be hard and sometimes humbling, but a major barometer of change is your commitment to being accountable. Many men who have told their stories in this book have indicated that staying violence-free is a life-long commitment. They are continually aware of how they interact with women to avoid backsliding into past abusive behavior. The following discussion about honesty in a new relation-ship took place in one of our men's groups.

Daniel: I don't see why I need to tell my partner about my past relationship with Jill. It's over. I want to get on with my life.

MaryAnn: What do the rest of you think?

Matthew: I told my new partner about my battering. In fact I tell her what I learn in these groups. She was a little surprised when I told her, but I'm glad that I did. I don't want to repeat what I did to Molly. I mean, I really want this relationship to work. I'm committed to being honest about everything with her, and her knowing about my past will help keep me honest.

If you are in a new relationship, you will be exploring each other in many ways. When you tell your new partner about your past abuse, she may not state all that she is thinking or feeling, and it may take time for her to sort through her reac-tions. It would not be unusual for her to be cautious or even test your commitment to being nonviolent. Your awareness of her need for caution can help establish trust in the relationship.

Some men living violence-free lives with women check in with their partner about how they have handled certain situ-ations, especially conflict. They want to know if their partner has felt fearful during a discussion. For instance, they may want to know if their body language or voice was intimidating, so that they can correct that behavior the next time there is a disagreement.

"It is important for me to know if Connie is afraid of me in any way, or if she feels I'm exhibiting past behaviors," said Don in one of our discussion. "She has told me that on certain occasions she has withdrawn or backed off because she could tell that I was getting irritated. It didn't feel good to hear that, but I need to know it if I'm going to continue to change."

Talking to Your Children about Your Violence

Children often assume the blame for things that go wrong in their families. I remember my parents having a big argument late one evening. I strained my ears to hear if it had anything to do with us kids. My immediate thought was that I had done something wrong. My next thoughts focused on whether my parents might get a divorce. I kept thinking how I might intervene. At six years of age, I felt responsible to make things right between them.

In families where there has been violence, children feel enormous responsibility and therefore guilt. And it is in these families that parents are unavailable, leaving children nowhere to turn and no one to talk to.

Some research indicates that in families where there has been domestic abuse toward a spouse, the risk that the children have been abused is higher than usual. (15) If you have been abusive to your children or think that your discipline is becoming abusive, seek help from mental health centers in your community.

Some of the men I interviewed indicated that they talked with their children about their violence. Their motivation was to apologize and assure their children that they were changing.

Look for an appropriate time to talk to your children, but never force them into talking. They may not be ready, and the experiences they have had with you and your violence may be too fresh and painful. They may not feel safe with you, and pressuring them to talk might cause further harm.

If you talk to your children, be honest. Explain that what occurred in the past was *your* responsibility. Reassure them that they were not to blame. Let them know that you are taking steps to change and that your past abusive behavior was wrong. Admitting your violence to your children will not be easy, but they will respect your honesty even if they cannot articulate a response.

When you make the decision to talk with your children, do not talk about your abusive behavior in a way that implies that your partner or ex-partner is equally responsible. In no way should you blame your partner. Too many parents have done grave damage to their children by pitting one parent against the other and forcing the children to take sides.

Remember, your children may not be ready to have this discussion. Smaller children especially may feel uncomfortable. Do not pressure them. It is far more important that your present behavior demonstrate the changes that you have committed to.

Beyond Personal Change: Educating the Community

"Never doubt that a small group of thoughtful and committed citizens can change the world. Indeed it's the only thing that ever has." — *Margaret Mead*

Many men have gone public with the fact that they were abusive. They make that decision for a variety of reasons. For some men, telling others of their abuse is a way of staying accountable. For others, the motivation is to help other men by sharing their experiences and their process of change. For yet others, going public is a way to participate in changing society by confronting the attitudes and beliefs that foster violence. Some men speak in schools or community clubs, do public service announcements, or volunteer to work with domestic violence programs. Some men teach their sons that violence is not the answer to conflicts.

I know one man who speaks at police training sessions on domestic assault in Minnesota about his years of battering. After listening to him, the police officers have a clearer understanding of the dynamics of an abusive relationship. As a result, they can intervene more effectively in these cases.

There are many ways we can address violence against

women in our community. Men can take a more active and visible role in confronting sexual and domestic assaults. We can join neighborhood crime watches, participate in anti-rape marches, and organize community meetings. We can initiate dialogue in our schools, churches, local governments, unions, professional association meetings, and community clubs. We can write letters to the newspaper and talk to our friends. We can publicly confront judges who refuse to take domestic abuse cases seriously. We can lobby our mayors, state legislators, and congress for tougher laws to protect women who have been abused.

As fathers, we can teach our sons and daughters that attitudes or behaviors that degrade girls and women in any way are wrong. We should be able to talk clearly and with conviction to our children. We can help shape their thinking about men, women, equality, and violence. We need to remind them that if they witness inappropriate behavior on the bus or in the school yard or park, they do not need to participate.

Men can *and should* take the initiative to confront violence in homes and communities because most violence is instigated by men. Women don't usually kill people; they perpetrate less than 15% of the homicides in the United States. When women do kill, it is often in their own defense, notes Angela Browne, author of *When Battered Women Kill*. (16) Gang violence, fights, and domestic and sexual assaults are by and large a male phenomenon. It should be our responsibility to put an end to it.

Women have struggled for years to end rape and domestic violence. They have organized movements, fought for resources, lobbied for legislation, and spoken out about the magnitude of these problems. Men who ally with these movements should support women's leadership. If you plan an event or seek funding for a program or an event, talk with and work with women's groups in your community.

I am convinced that we can make a difference. I believe we will see more and more men speaking out and confronting sexism and men's violence. We can make a difference today, so that future generations will not have to experience the violence and abuse that occurs in homes throughout this country.

Staying on Course: Your Life-long Commitment

"I had promised my wife Kathy that I would never hit her again. I really made an effort to apply the things I had learned in my group and the self-control techniques I had worked on. I was determined not to repeat my past behavior. We were having an argument about something, and I leaned across the table and yelled, 'Now you listen!' She was startled and I was kind of shocked that I did it. I felt the same rush like I used to feel when I battered her and I was aware of her fear. I saw how easy it would be for me to slip back into old behaviors." — *Earl*

Drifting back into familiar patterns of responding to conflict, anger, and agitation with an abusive act is a real danger for men who have used violence in the past. The instantaneous response to an abusive act and the subsequent power one achieves can be intoxicating. The conflict ends, and it ends on your terms.

Most of the men I interviewed for this book said that they work continually to avoid backsliding. Whenever they felt hurt, jealous, or angry, their first thoughts were to react in a way that would bring an immediate response. Being intimidating was so much a part of how they handled conflict that it was almost an automatic reaction. In the past, yelling or grabbing their partners would make their partners afraid and put them on the defensive. If they resisted, these men could always resort to more violence.

To avoid this all-too-familiar path, men who lead violence-free lives practice some of the exercises outlined in this book. They maintain a persevering attitude of self-control. There can be no "slips," like an alcoholic going off the wagon for a night.

Am I asking for perfection? No. I am asking only that you remain nonviolent and that you monitor yourself to determine if you are using abusive behaviors.

Remember, acknowledging positive and healthy responses to problems and conflict resolution is important, too. Do not underestimate your achievements. The new path you are taking for yourself as a changing man is important.

For those of you who are still with the partner that you

abused, you should be especially aware of your response to disagreements. Your partner's fears may stay with her for a long time. If you are in a new relationship and you have told your new partner about your history, she may also be hesitant or nervous when you get upset or angry. Getting feedback from her can be helpful. Your partner, however, is under no obligation to give you this feedback. If she feels safe and is willing, be certain to take advantage of her help.

Part of your commitment to staying nonviolent may involve exposing yourself to new ideas and challenges about masculinity and the socialization that shapes men and women. Your new awareness can open doors to a different way to view the world and interact with others. Changing men try to share their lives with others. They become active, not only to contribute, but also to keep growing on a personal level.

Your commitment to change cannot be temporary; it must become part of who you are. At first, there may not be much support from friends, family, or coworkers. But you will know that your new path is the right one to be walking down. You will feel better about yourself.

Try to be a true friend to other men. When you see or sense that a friend or family member is being abusive to a partner, make it your business to intervene. Choose an appropriate time to talk to that person and strongly encourage him to get help. Use your own experience as a guide; tell your story and tell him what you know. He may reject your attempts, but you may also plant a seed, which may be nurtured when he is ready to confront his problems. You can be understanding but also be honest.

Lastly, do not be afraid to seek help. You should not feel ashamed of seeing a counselor to work on issues that come up in your life. If you were physically sick, you would not hesitate to see a doctor. A therapist or counselor can be a good neutral party to talk to, and asking for help is not a sign of weakness but an acknowledgment of your desire to be healthy and in balance. If you feel depressed at times, have trouble coping with or resolving problems, stress out, or feel stuck, seek help. Attend a support group or consciousness-raising group. If there is none in your community, organize one.

As you change, you will soon recognize the rewards. Your relationships will change and you will feel differently about yourself. When you make this life-long commitment, you are making a personal statement about who you are and your capacity to change. Will you make mistakes? Sure you will. But your willingness to learn from your mistakes and grow will make the journey you have started more valuable as you reach your goal.

Conclusion

"A journey of a thousand miles must begin
with a single step." — *Lao-tzu: The Way of Lao-tzu*

Violence gives a man who batters temporary power and control over his partner. He ends an argument, vents his anger, or punishes. But at what cost? Although he often gets his way, he also hurts and destroys in the process. Violence and abusive behavior become a cancer, consuming the victim and perpetrator alike, and usually killing the relationship.

Men who batter try to justify their behavior, yet the terror in their partner's eyes is always there as a reminder that they— and no one else—have done something hurtful and abusive. Men who batter say, "I don't understand," but they do. There *is* no excuse. In their attempt to avoid responsibility they dig in their heels and try not to feel or remember. They turn on a kind of psychic numbing to have peace within themselves. A friend once told me that men who batter look in the mirror, see that their face is dirty, and wipe the mirror to get it clean. Yet, some men *do* face the problem head on and make commitments to change. You have met some of these men in this book.

And what of the women in this book? They are survivors. They have struggled to understand all that has happened and they are healing. I try and imagine how they must have felt as the blows and kicks bruised their bodies. What were they thinking when they saw the rage and hatred in their partner's eyes? They must have wondered how the men they chose with love as partners and husbands could do these horrible things. Were their spirits broken? Would they ever trust a man again?

I also wonder about the children of the men and women in this book. Have they already been infected by what they have witnessed? Will I see their sons in future groups for men who batter, or will the cycle be broken with this generation?

Much of this book has been about men taking personal responsibility for past behavior. These men have learned not to blame others and have reached a state of awareness so that positive change can take place. How many men will take the initiative? Many will enter new relationships and remain non-violent. Many will not learn from the past and will be doomed to repeat it.

At times, over the years, I have been discouraged working in this field. I thought that with new laws and increased societal awareness domestic violence would be on the wane, but it is not. Domestic homicides are a daily occurrence. Emergency rooms continue receiving victims. And the little secrets in so many of our homes continue to mask the pain.

Yet, through it all, I remain hopeful. Many men who have battered have made significant changes. They have grown and recognized how their past beliefs and attitudes toward women have contaminated their relationships and led to violence. They have seen the hurt they were causing and have said, "No more!" With the help of programs and concerned people, they were able to change. They still struggle, but they are personally rewarded for their commitment to living a nonviolent life.

Now that you have completed this book, don't stop here. Set some goals for your life and practice what you have learned. Ask for help. Use the exercises in this book to keep you focused on your objectives. *You will change, if you want to change.* Today you can make some serious commitments about how you want to lead your life. You won't regret your decision.

Appendix

The following text and forms may be useful as handouts for counselors and group leaders, and may be reproduced. The page numbers on which they appear in the book are in parentheses below.

Power and Control Wheel (page 81)

Equality Wheel (page 136)

Guidelines for Remaining Nonviolent (page 99)

Time-out Rules (page 117)

The Negotiation Guide (page 151)

Power and Control Wheel

Using Coercion and Threats Making and/or carrying out threats to do something to hurt her • threatening to leave her, to commit suicide, to report her to welfare • making her drop charges • making her do illegal things

Using Intimidation Making her afraid by using looks, actions, gestures • smashing things • destroying her property • abusing pets • displaying weapons

Using Emotional Abuse Putting her down • making her feel bad about herself • calling her names • making her think she's crazy • playing mind games • humiliating her • making her feel guilty

Using Isolation Controlling what she does, who she sees and talks to, what she reads, where she goes • limiting her outside involvement • using jealousy to justify actions

Denying, Minimizing, and Blaming Making light of the abuse and not taking her concerns about it seriously • saying the abuse didn't happen • shifting responsibility for abusive behavior • saying she caused it

Using Children Making her feel guilty about the children • using the children to relay messages • using visitation to harass her • threatening to take the children away

Using Male Privilege Treating her like a servant • making all the big decisions • acting like the "master of the castle" • being the one to define men's and women's roles

Using Economic Abuse Preventing her from getting or keeping a job • making her ask for money • giving her an allowance • taking her money • not letting her know or have access to family income

Equality Wheel

Negotiation and Fairness Seeking mutually satisfying resolutions to conflict • accepting change • being willing to compromise

Nonthreatening behavior Talking and acting so that she feels safe and comfortable expressing herself and doing things

Respect Listening to her nonjudgmentally • being emotionally affirming and understanding • valuing opinions

Trust and Support Supporting her goals in life • respecting her right to her own feelings, friends, activities, and opinions

Honesty and Accountability Accepting responsibility for self • acknowledging past use of violence • admitting being wrong • communicating openly and truthfully

Responsible Parenting Sharing parental responsibilities • being a positive nonviolent role model for the children

Shared Responsibilities Mutually agreeing on a fair distribution of work • making family decisions together

Economic Partnership Making money decisions together • making sure both partners benefit from financial arrangements

Guidelines for Remaining Nonviolent

I, _____ , accept and commit to the
following principles:

1. Violence is not okay unless I am truly in fear of being hurt,
   and then I should only use as much force as I need to defend
   myself.

2. In the future, I will be aware of flashpoints—issues or
   situations where I become agitated or very angry—which in
   the past have prompted violence by me or my partner.

3. I will leave situations (take a time-out) rather than use
   violence.

4. I will accept the fact that my use of violence is based on my
   desire to control a situation. I do not always need to be in
   control, to be proven right, or to win.

5. I will strive toward respectful resolutions of conflicts without being abusive.

_____   _____
(Name)   (Counselor)

Time-out Rules

1. Take a time-out when you recognize your cues and before your anger level escalates.

2. Take a time-out when you feel like you want to become abusive; do not take a time-out to avoid conflict.

3. Tell your partner you are taking a time-out.

4. Tell your partner how long you will be gone.

5. Do not drink, use drugs, or drive.

6. Call a friend or group member for support.

7. Do calming exercises like walking, shooting free throws at a basketball court, or meditating.

8. Think positive thoughts. Do not dwell on the problem that caused you to become angry.

9. If you are still agitated and need more time than you agreed to, call your partner and let her know.

10. Your partner is not obliged to take a time-out; you take a time-out for *yourself.*

11. If your partner indicates that she is afraid of you, stay away. Find an alternative place to stay until things have calmed down.

12. When you return, do not insist that you and your partner should solve or resolve the conflict you were having.

13. If you notice your cues again, take another time-out.

14. Whenever you follow the time-out rules, make a note of the positive way you handled the situation and its results.

An important note: If you are going to use time-outs in your relationship, review this section and the previous one with your partner. You may want to practice a time-out when you are not angry so that you and your partner understand the process and each other's expectations. Your partner needs to know the rules of the time-out so she knows what to expect.

The Negotiation Guide

1. Regardless of how angry or hurt I feel I will remain nonviolent.

2. If I disagree with my partner's position I will still be respectful toward her.

3. I will remain seated during the discussion.

4. I will not yell, scream, or use my voice in an intimidating manner.

5. I will not threaten my partner in any way.

6. I will not use put-downs, call my partner names, or be sarcastic or belittling.

7. I will not bring up past incidents to prove a point.

8. I will avoid blaming or shaming statements.

9. I will strive not to get defensive.

10. I will listen to my partner's position and refrain from interrupting.

11. I will commit to work toward a compromise.

12. I will be willing to explore my own issues and take responsibility for mistakes I have made.

13. I will respect my partner's wishes to end the discussion.

14. I will be honest.

15. I will talk about my feelings but will not use them as a way to manipulate my partner.

Notes

1. Michael Paymar and Ellen Pence, *Education Groups for Men Who Batter* (New York: Springer Publishing Company, 1993).

2. Murray Arnold Straus, Richard J. Gelles, and Suzanne K. Steinmetz, *Behind Closed Doors: Violence in the American Family* (New York: Anchor Press/Doubleday, 1980).

3. Rebecca Emerson Dobash and Russell Dobash, *Violence against Wives* (New York: The Free Press, 1983).

4. Jane O'Reilly, "Wife Beating: The Silent Crime," in *Time* magazine (September 1983).

5. Paulo Freire, *Pedagogy of the Oppressed* (New York: Continuum, 1992).

6. Dobash and Dobash, *Violence against Wives*.

7. A. Rosenbaum and K.O. O'Leary, "Children: The Unintended Victims of Marital Violence," in *American Journal of Orthopsychiatry* Volume 51, 1981.

8. Anne L. Ganley, *Treating Men who Batter: Theory, Practice, and Programs* in P. Lynn Caesar and L. Kevin Hamberger, editors (New York: Springer Publishing Company, 1989).

9. Barbara Hart, *Safety for Women: Monitoring Batterers' Programs* (Harrisburg, PA: Pennsylvania Coalition Against Domestic Violence, 1988).

10. Ellen Pence and Michael Paymar, *Power and Control Tactics of Men who Batter* (Duluth, MN: Control Log, 1985).

11. Peter G. Jaffe, David A. Wolfe, and edited by Susan K. Wilson, *Children of Battered Women* (Newbury Park, CA: Sage Publications, 1990).

12. Freire, *Pedagogy of the Oppressed.*

13. Power and Control Wheel (Duluth, MN: Duluth Domestic Abuse Intervention Project, 1985).

14. Equality Wheel (Duluth, MN: Duluth Domestic Abuse Intervention Project, 1985).

15. Lenore Walker, *The Battered Woman* (New York: Harper and Row, 1979).

16. Angela Browne, *When Battered Women Kill* (New York: The Free Press, 1984).

Resource Hotlines and Organizations

The following resources may be useful for men, women, and practitioners reading this book. Most states and many provinces in Canada have organizations that provide referral information for victims and perpetrators of domestic violence. Some of the organizations listed may be able to recommend services or programs in your community.

State Toll-free Domestic Violence Hotlines

Arkansas	(800) 332-4443
Nevada	(800) 334-7233
New Hampshire	(800) 852-3311
New Jersey	(800) 572-7233
New York (English)	(800) 942-9606
New York (Spanish)	(800) 942-6908
North Dakota	(800) 472-2911
Oklahoma	(800) 522-7233
Washington State	(800) 562-6025
Wisconsin	(800) 333-7233

Child Abuse

Military Family Resource Center (Toll-free)   (800) 336-4592
(703) 696-5806

Publishes the *Military Family* newspaper and operates the Military Family Clearinghouse, which provides information and services to military families.

National Child Abuse Hotline (Toll-free)   (800) 422-4453

Parents Anonymous (Toll-free)   (800) 421-0353

National Organizations

Center for the Prevention of Sexual and Domestic Violence
1914 North 34th Street, Suite 105
Seattle WA 98103   (206) 634-1903

The Family Violence Prevention Fund
Building One, Suite 200
1001 Potrero Avenue
San Francisco CA 94110   (415) 821-4553
Provides comprehensive services to victims of domestic violence, advocacy, training and technical assistance, public education, and public policy reform.

The Family Violence Project
Building One, Suite 200
1001 Potrero Avenue
San Francisco CA 94110   (415) 821-4553
Provides extensive legal and court advocacy to victims of felony
domestic assault, including crisis intervention, case assessment,
monitoring cases, and preparing court orders.

National Clearinghouse for the Defense of Battered Women
125 South 9th Street, Suite 302
Philadelphia PA 19107   (215) 351-0010

National Coalition Against Domestic Violence
P.O. Box 34103
Washington DC 20043-4103   (202) 638-6388

National Coalition Against Domestic Violence
P.O. Box 18749
Denver CO 80218-074   (303) 839-1852
Provides information to battered women on programs and services throughout the country on domestic violence issues.

National Organization For Men Against Sexism (NOMAS)
54 Mint Street, Suite 300
San Francisco CA 94103   (415) 546-6627
Publishes *Changing Men,* a magazine about masculinity and
men's issues, and promotes activities to end men's violence and
confront sexism.

National Training Project
206 West Fourth Street
Duluth MN 55806   (218) 722-2781
Provides on-site training and technical assistance for the criminal justice system, law enforcement, mental health practitioners,
and advocates for battered women in the United States and
Canada. Also provides training on the Duluth model for working with men who batter.

National Organization For Changing Men/BrotherPeace
P.O. Box 451
Watseka IL 60970
Promotes social change activities for men working to end vio-
lence against women.

The Oakland Men's Project (OMP)
440 Grand Avenue
Oakland CA 94610   (510) 835-2433
Conducts educational workshops and community organizing
and training activities to empower adults and young people to
stop violence.

Recommended Domestic Abuse Programs Providing Services for Men

The following is a partial listing of recommended programs. All
of these resources provide local or statewide services for men
who batter, unless otherwise noted. Many of them also provide
resources for battered women.

For a more complete list, the Ending Men's Violence Task

Force publishes and distributes the *Ending Men's Violence National Referral Directory*. This directory lists programs that provide services throughout the country to men who batter. You can receive a copy of the directory by calling (314) 725-6137.

Advocate Program
1515 NW 7th Street, Suite 112
Miami FL 33125   (305) 642-6867
Provides services to English- and Spanish-speaking men who batter.

Alternatives to Violence
P.O. Box 909
Wailuku HI 96793   (808) 242-9559

Alternatives to Violence
P.O. Box 10448
Hilo HI 96721-0612   (808) 969-7798

Alternatives to Violence
3094 Elua Street
Lihue, Kauai, HI 96766   (808) 245-5959

AMEND   (303) 832-6363
Provides services in the metropolitan Denver area.

Center For Non-Violence
235 West Creighton
Fort Wayne IN 46802   (219) 422-8082

Common Purpose Inc.
259 Massachusetts Avenue
Arlington MA 02174   (617) 641-3101

Common Purpose Inc.
P.O. Box 88
Jamaica Plain, MA 02174
Provides services to English- and Spanish-speaking men.

Domestic Abuse Intervention Project
206 West Fourth Street
Duluth MN 55806   (218) 722-2781

EMERGE
18 Hurley Street
Cambridge MA 02141   (617) 422-7690

House of Ruth
2201 Asgonne Drive
Baltimore MD 21218   (410) 889-0840
Coordinates *The Batterer's Program*, which provides services in
the Baltimore area to men who batter.

ManAlive Marin County
345 Johnstone Drive
San Rafael CA 94903   (415) 499-1500
24-Hour hotline: (415) 924-1070
Provides services in the San Francisco Bay Area to English- and
Spanish-speaking men who batter; provides programs for prisons.

Men Stopping Violence Inc.
1025 DeKalb Avenue, #25
Atlanta GA 30307   (404) 688-1376

Men Overcoming Violence (MOVE)
54 Mint Street, Suite 300
San Francisco CA 94103   (415) 777-4496

NOVA
1205 Harding Place
Charlotte NC 28204   (704) 336-4344

ONEIDA Tribal Social Services Domestic Abuse Program (Project Medicine Wheel)
P.O. Box 365
Oneida WI 54155   (414) 869-4415
Provides services to Native American men who batter.

PEACE
211 Union Street, Suite 626
Nashville TN 37201   (615) 255-0711

RAVEN (Rape and Violence End Now)
P.O. Box 24159
St. Louis MO 63130   (314) 725-6137

St. Cloud Intervention Project
915 1st Street So., Suite 14
St. Cloud MN 56301   (612) 251-7203

Milwaukee Domestic Abuse Intervention Project
Milwaukee Court House
901 North 9th Street, Room 711
Milwaukee WI 53233   (414) 278-4679

Vera House
P.O. Box 365
Syracuse NY 13209   (315) 425-0901

Training and Technical Assistance

The Empowerment Project
1130 Harding Place, Suite 2
Charlotte NC 28203
Provides training on domestic violence issues in the African-American community.

Mending The Sacred Hoop
206 West Fourth Street
Duluth MN 55806   (218) 722-3414
Provides training and technical assistance for working with
tribal government and addressing family violence issues in the
Native-American community.

The National Training Project
206 West Fourth Street
Duluth MN 55806   (218) 722-2781
Provides training and technical assistance on policy development and development of intervention programs.

Pennsylvania Coalition Legal Office
524 McKight Street
Reading PA 19601   (215) 373-5697
Addresses legal and policy issues related to domestic violence.

Programs and Assistance for Gays and Lesbians

Community United Against Violence
973 Market Street, Suite 500
San Francisco CA 94103   (415) 777-5500

Community University Health Care Center
201 Bloomington Avenue South
Minneapolis MN 55404   (612) 627-4774

Men Overcoming Violence (MOVE)
(See page 195 for listing)

National Gay and Lesbian Task Force
1734 14th Street, NW   (202) 332-6483
Washington DC 20009-4309   (202) 332-0207
24-Hour Hotline: (415) 333-HELP

N.Y. City Gay and Lesbian Anti-Violence Project
1208 West 13th Street
New York NY 10011
24-Hour Hotline   (212) 807-0197

Seattle Counseling Service For Sexual Minorities
200 West Mercer, Suite 300
Seattle WA 98119   (206) 282-9307

Recommended Books, Manuals, and Films

Books

Ain't I a Woman: Black Women and Feminism by bell hooks (Boston, Massachusetts: South End Press, 1981).

Backlash: The Undeclared War Against American Women by Susan Faludi (New York: Crown Publishers, 1991).

Battered Wives by Del Martin, revised edition (Volcano, CA: Volcano Press, 1981).

Education Groups For Men Who Batter: The Duluth Model by Michael Paymar and Ellen Pence (New York: Springer Publishing Company, 1993). Order from: (218) 722-2781.

Men's Work: How to Stop the Violence That Tears Our Lives Apart by Paul Kivel (New York: Hazelden/Ballantine, 1992).

Men Who Batter: An Integrated Approach for Stopping Wife Abuse by Edward Gondolf (Holmes Beach, FL: Learning Publications, 1985).

Pedagogy of the Oppressed by Paulo Freire (New York: Continuum, 1992).

Violence Against Wives by R. Emerson Dobash and Russell P. Dobash (New York: The Free Press, 1983). An historical analysis of wife assault.

When Love Goes Wrong: What to Do When You Can't Do Anything Right—Strategies for Women with Controlling Partners by Susan Schechter and Ann Jones (New York: HarperCollins, 1992). Order from: (800) 331-3761. An important book for battered women.

Women and Male Violence: The Visions and Struggles of the Battered Women's Movement by Susan Schechter (Boston, MA: South End Press, 1982).

Manuals and Curriculums

The Justice System Response To Domestic Assault Cases: A Guide For Policy Development by Ellen Pence with Michael Paymar, Coral McDonnell and Madeline Duprey. Order from: National Training Project, 206 West Fourth Street, Duluth MN 55806; (218) 722-2781.

Learning To Live Without Violence: A Handbook for Men by Daniel J. Sonkin and Michael Durphy, updated edition (Volcano, CA: Volcano Press, 1989). Order from: Volcano Press (209) 296-3445.

Learning To Live Without Violence: A Worktape for Men by Daniel J. Sonkin and Michael Durphy (Volcano, CA: Volcano Press, 1989). An audio cassette adaptation, 115 minutes. Order from: Volcano Press (209) 296-3445.

Power and Control: Tactics of Men Who Batter by Michael Paymar and Ellen Pence. Order from: National Training Project, 206 West Fourth Street, Duluth MN 55806; (218) 722-2781.

Safety for Women: Monitoring Batterers' Programs by Barbara Hart. Order from: Pennsylvania Coalition Against Domestic Violence, 6400 Flank Drive, Gateway Corporate Center, Suite 1300, Harrisburg PA; (800) 537-2238.

Wife Abuse in the Armed Forces by Lois West, W. Turner, and Ellen Dunwoody. Order from: Center for Women's Studies, 2000 P Street NW, Suite 508, Washington DC 20036.

Wife Assault: A Training Manual for Counselors and Advocates by Debra Sinclair. (Toronto, Ontario: Ontario Publications, 1985). Order from: (800) 268-7540.

Films

Battered, directed by Lee Grant. Order from: Joseph Feury Productions, Inc., 120 Riverside Drive, New York NY 10024. A dramatic look at the experiences and feelings of women who have been battered.

Men's Lives. Order from: New Day Films, P.O. Box 315, Franklin Lakes NJ 07417. Examines male socialization.

Profile of an Assailant. Order from: National Training Project, 206 West Fourth Street, Duluth MN 55806; (218) 722-2781. A candid discussion with a man who battered, and the experiences of battered women are highlighted in this film. This film is useful for training and programs for men who batter.

Time Out Series: Deck The Halls, Up The Creek, Shifting Gears. Order from: ODN Productions, 74 Varick Street, New York NY 10013. Short films designed for programs for men who batter.

To Have and to Hold. Order from: New Day Films, P.O. Box 315, Franklin Lake NJ 07417. Useful for support groups for battered women and programs for men who batter.

Index

liberation by, 163
as long process, 163
children (see also personal stories)
discussion of violence, 176
effect of violence on, 72, 110,
176
reaction to violence, 162
used to control partner, 71–75
choice, violence as personal, 40
"self-defense", 96–100
anger, 105
change, 155
commitment, long-term, 179–81
community, educating about violence, 177–78
conflict, resolution, 127–57
control
basis of jealousy, 121
economic, 148
by intimidation, 62
object of violence, 62
reaction to, 23
self-defeating, 70
use of money for, 23
wheel diagram, 81
counseling, after violence
controlled, 39

D

dating, honesty in, 174–76
denial, 86–107
by avoiding responsibility, 86
by rationalization, 92
rebound relationship as, 131
of responsibility, 91–94
directory, of programs for the batterer, 194
Dobash, Rebecca, 38
Dobash, Russell, 38
domination
cause of violence, 7
root of violence, 80, 130, 156
drugs (see personal stories for mix-

ture of violence, alcohol,
and drugs)

E

economic abuse, 81
economic control, 148
egalitarian relationship, 133–38
Equality Wheel, 135–36, 185
excuses for violence, 94, 102
exercise
handling money problems, 143–
45
health and balance, 172–74
learning about violence, 41–44
negotiating roles, 138–40
self-talk, 120
using abusive behavior, 81–84
weekly inventory, 84–85
why use violence, 47–49

F

feelings
battering to relieve, 149
benefits of discussing, 168
as control tactic, 147, 150
male suppression of, 146, 168
socializing males against, 149
feminine qualities
male fear of, 22
male rejection of, 22
Freire, Paulo, 29, 77
frequency of violent behavior, 1

G

gangs breed violence, 20

H

Hart, Barbara, 40
healing, 157–82
slowness of, 80
time required, 35

Also from Hunter House Publishers

**HELPING TEENS STOP VIOLENCE: A Practical Guide
for Counselors, Educators, and Parents**
by Allan Creighton, Battered Women's Alternatives
with Paul Kivel, Oakland Men's Project

*"We believe individual acts of violence are expressions of much
broader patterns of social violence, and that social violence is an
expression of long-standing power imbalances between 'have'
and 'have not' groups in our society. What we see from day to
day are the high percentage of individuals involved; what we
rarely hear about are the broader imbalances that motivate the
violence . . . ."* — **From the book**

Today's teenagers live in a violent world. They are subject
to abuse at home, at school, and in social situations. For
the past fourteen years, the nationally acclaimed Oakland
Men's Project (OMP) and Battered Women's Alternatives
(BWA) have been conducting seminars and workshops
with teens and adults around the country, weaving issues
of gender, race, age, and sexual orientation into frank
discussions about male violence and its roots.

This new book by the founders of OMP and BWA
provides guidelines on how to help teenagers help
themselves out of the cycle of abuse. Their program
provides the groundwork for working with teens to
reduce the violence in their lives and in the world around
them. Topics include:

- How to initiate discussions with teens about
  violence and uncover its root causes
- How role plays can aid in exploring issues of race,
  gender, and sexual orientation
- How to help teens set up peer support groups
- What steps to follow when helping abused teens

*"Beyond the role play, the support group, and the trained
volunteers, this educational process pictures adults and young
people finding a common cause, common language, and a
common understanding to face the very real conditions that
limit us all."*
— *Family Violence & Sexual Assault Bulletin*

168 pages ... paperback $11.95 ... spiral bound $14.95

To order, please see last page

Other Books from Hunter House Publishers

RECLAIMING YOUR FUTURE: Finding Your Path After Recovery by Kendall Johnson, Ph.D.

Recovery is a stepping stone to a better life, not a substitute for it. This book helps those who have dealt with addiction and codependency issues take the second most important step: reclaiming their lost promise, recreating the rest of their life. The book describes how to get past common stumbling blocks in the twelve-step approach, resolve past crises and family issues, and learn to understand your needs and explore your full potential. An important book for anyone who wants to move *beyond* recovery and experience real spiritual and emotional growth.

208 pages ... paperback ... $10.95

WHEN SOMEONE YOU LOVE IS IN THERAPY
by Michael Gold, Ph.D., with Marie Scampini

Explains the ins and outs of therapy to those whose loved ones are going through it, and answers such questions as "Why did they go into therapy?" "What goes on there?" "How do I know if something goes wrong?" and "What about me?" This book demystifies psychotherapy and shows readers how to cope with their *own* feelings—their questions, fears, anxieties, and insecurities—so they can feel confident themselves and be supportive of their loved one.

208 pages ... paperback ... $10.95

WRITING FROM WITHIN: A Unique Guide to Writing Your Life's Stories by Bernard Selling

Telling your life stories can be a voyage of self-discovery, freeing up images and thought that have long remained hidden. Completely updated to reflect the author's current teaching methods, this book will show readers how to write stirring, detailed portraits of their experiences which are both therapeutic today and valued as memorable stories for generations to come.

"Anyone who has ever lost the opportunity to find out what really mattered to an important friend or relative will respond instantly to this book." — *Booklist*

288 pages ... paperback ... $11.95

Call for our free catalog at 1-800-266-5592

Other Books from Hunter House Publishers

CAPTIVE HEARTS, CAPTIVE MINDS: Freedom and Recovery from Cults and Abusive Relationships
by Madeleine Landau Tobias and Janja Lalich

People in a cult or abusive one-on-one relationship suffer from fear, depression, confusion, low self-esteem, and posttraumatic stress. This book provides the hands-on help they need to recover from manipulation and controlling behavior. It includes personal stories of healing and recovery; sections on family issues, violence, and sexual abuse; and an extensive list of resources and organizations. CAPTIVE HEARTS, CAPTIVE MINDS offers victims and their families a renewed sense of trust and hope for a life beyond the cult experience.

320 pages ... paperback $14.95 ... also available in hardcover

EVERYDAY RACISM: Reports from Women of Two Cultures by Philomena Essed, Ph.D.

In this important book, two different cultures are explored to illuminate significant truths about hidden racism in everyday interactions. Extensive interviews with Surinamese women in Amsterdam, the Netherlands, and African-American women in Oakland, California show the constructive difference an oral and shared history of fighting racism can make. EVERYDAY RACISM is for all people seeking to define their values, establish their identities, and fulfill their struggle against bigotry.

304 pages ... paperback $12.95 ... also available in hardcover

SPIRIT OF CHANGE: Voices of Hope for a World in Crisis by Christopher Titmuss

A series of interviews with such notables as Ram Dass, J. Krishnamurti, Fritjof Capra, and Thich Nhat Hanh, as well as interviews with remarkable everyday people about what needs to be done for the health, welfare, and liberation of the planet. It is a chronicle of the kind of constructive difference one person can make in a world in crisis, at a time when hope is in short supply.

"In a time when despair can lead us to apathy, this anthology offers a vision of hope—and an inspiration to action."
— *Yoga Journal*

224 pages ... paperback ... $9.95

See over for ordering and discounts

ORDER FORM

10% DISCOUNT on orders of $20 or more —
20% DISCOUNT on orders of $50 or more —
30% DISCOUNT on orders of $250 or more —
On cost of books for fully prepaid orders

NAME

ADDRESS

CITY/STATE   ZIP/POSTCODE

PHONE   COUNTRY (outside USA)

TITLE	QTY	PRICE	TOTAL
Captive Hearts, Captive Minds	| @	$ 14.95	
Everyday Racism	| @	$ 12.95	
Helping Teens Stop Violence *(paperback)*	| @	$ 11.95	
Helping Teens Stop Violence *(spiral)*	| @	$ 14.95	
Reclaiming Your Future	| @	$ 10.95	
Spirit of Change	| @	$ 9.95	
Violent No More *(paperback)*	| @	$ 10.95	
Violent No More *(hardcover)*	| @	$ 19.95	
When Someone You Love Is in Therapy	| @	$ 10.95	
Writing From Within	| @	$ 11.95	

Shipping costs:
First book: $2.50
($3.50 for Canada)
Each additional book:
$.75 ($1.00 for Canada)
For UPS rates and bulk orders call us at (510) 865-5282

TOTAL	
Less discount @_____%	(_____)
TOTAL COST OF BOOKS	
Calif. residents add sales tax	
Shipping & handling	
TOTAL ENCLOSED	
Please pay in U.S. funds only	

❏ Check   ❏ Money Order   ❏ Visa   ❏ M/C

Card # _____ Exp date _____

Signature _____

Complete and mail to

Hunter House Inc., Publishers
PO Box 2914, Alameda CA 94501-0914
Orders: 1-800-266-5592
Phone (510) 865-5282 Fax (510) 865-4295
❏ Check here to receive our book catalog

VNM 8/94